First World War
and Army of Occupation
War Diary
France, Belgium and Germany

56 DIVISION
Headquarters, Branches and Services
General Staff
1 March 1917 - 31 March 1917

WO95/2933/2

The Naval & Military Press Ltd
www.nmarchive.com
Published in association with The National Archives

Published by

The Naval & Military Press Ltd

Unit 10 Ridgewood Industrial Park,

Uckfield, East Sussex,

TN22 5QE England

Tel: +44 (0) 1825 749494

www.naval-military-press.com

www.nmarchive.com

This diary has been reprinted in facsimile from the original. Any imperfections are inevitably reproduced and the quality may fall short of modern type and cartographic standards.

© **Crown Copyright**
Images reproduced by permission of The National Archives, London, England, 2015.

Contents

Document type	Place/Title	Date From	Date To
Heading	56th Divn G.S. March 17. Vol 14		
Heading	War Diary of General Staff Hd-Qrs 56th Division From 1st March 1917 To 31st March 1917 Vol 14		
War Diary	Lagorgue	01/03/1917	05/03/1917
War Diary	Willeman	06/03/1917	07/03/1917
War Diary	Le Cauroy	08/03/1917	31/03/1917
Operation(al) Order(s)	56th Division Order No. 70 Appendix A	03/03/1917	03/03/1917
Miscellaneous	Appendix A.		
Miscellaneous	Amendments To 56th Div. Order No. 69.	03/03/1917	03/03/1917
Operation(al) Order(s)	56th Division Order No. 71.	06/03/1917	06/03/1917
Miscellaneous	March Table Issued With 56th Div. Order No. 71.		
Miscellaneous	Appendix "A" Flers Area. Brigade Billeting Areas.		
Miscellaneous	A Form. Messages And Signals.		
Operation(al) Order(s)	56th Division Order No. 72.	08/03/1917	08/03/1917
Operation(al) Order(s)	56th Division Order No. 73.	11/03/1917	11/03/1917
Map	Map Showing Divisional Areas		
Miscellaneous	Relief & March Table Attached To 56th Div. Order No. 73, Dated March 11th 1917.		
Miscellaneous	Amendment to 56th Div. Order No. 73	12/03/1917	12/03/1917
Miscellaneous	A Form. Messages And Signals.		
Operation(al) Order(s)	56th Division Order No. 74.	18/03/1917	18/03/1917
Map			
Operation(al) Order(s)	56th Divisional Order No. 75.	18/03/1917	18/03/1917
Operation(al) Order(s)	56th Divisional Order No. 76.	22/03/1917	22/03/1917
Miscellaneous	March Table Issued With 56th Division Order No. 76.		
Miscellaneous	56th Division. G.A.43.	20/03/1917	20/03/1917
Map	Neuville Vitasse		
Miscellaneous	VII Corps Appreciation And Instructions.	19/03/1917	19/03/1917
Miscellaneous	56th Division Instructions. Action Of Massed Machine Guns.	29/03/1917	29/03/1917
Miscellaneous	56th Divn. No.G.A.58.	24/03/1917	24/03/1917
Miscellaneous			
Miscellaneous	Situation Map VII Corps South Sector.		
Operation(al) Order(s)	56th Division. Warning Order No. 77.	22/03/1917	22/03/1917
Map			
Operation(al) Order(s)	56th Division Order No. 78.	28/03/1917	28/03/1917
Miscellaneous	March Table Issued With 56th Division Order No. 78.		
Miscellaneous	Amendment To 56th Division Order No. 78.	29/03/1917	29/03/1917
Miscellaneous	Location Table.		
Miscellaneous	Location Table Appendix B		
Map			
Map	Location Table		
Miscellaneous	56th Divisional Tactical Progress Report No. 126. Appendix C	01/03/1917	01/03/1917
Miscellaneous	56th Divisional Tactical Progress Report No. 127. from 8.0 a.m. 1st March to 8.0 a.m. 2nd March 1917.	02/03/1917	02/03/1917
Miscellaneous	56th Divisional Tactical Progress Report No. 128. from 8.0 a.m. 2nd March to 8.0 a.m. 3rd March, 1917.	03/03/1917	03/03/1917
Miscellaneous	56th Divisional Tactical Progress Report No. 129. from 8.0 a.m. 3rd March to 8.0 a.m. 4th March, 1917.	04/03/1917	04/03/1917

Miscellaneous	56th Divisional Tactical Progress Report No. 130. from 8.0 a.m. 4th March to 8.0 a.m. 5th March, 1917.	05/02/1917	05/02/1917
Miscellaneous	56th Divisional Tactical Progress Report No. 1 From 5 p.m. 20th March to 5. p.m. 21st March, 1917.	22/03/1917	22/03/1917
Miscellaneous	56th Divisional Tactical Progress Report No. 2 From 5 a.m. 22nd March to 5. a.m. 23 March, 1917.	24/03/1917	24/03/1917
Miscellaneous	56th Divisional Tactical Progress Report No. 3 From 5.0 a.m. 23rd March to 5.0 a.m. 24th March 1917.	24/03/1917	24/03/1917
Miscellaneous	56th Divisional Artillery. Summary of Intelligence For 24 Hours Ending Noon 24.3.17.		
Miscellaneous	Report On Hostile Artillery Fire.		
Miscellaneous	56th Divisional Tactical Progress Report No. 5. From 5 p.m. 24th March to 5 p.m. 25th March, 1917	26/03/1917	26/03/1917
Miscellaneous	Report On Our Artillery.		
Miscellaneous	Report On Hostile Artillery. From. 12 noon 25.3.17 to 12 noon 26.3.17.		
Miscellaneous	56th Divisional Tactical Progress Report No. 4. From 5.0 p.m. 23rd March to 5.0 p.m. 24th March, 1917.	25/03/1917	25/03/1917
Miscellaneous	Report On Hostile Artillery Fire. From 12 Noon 24.3.17 To 12 Noon 25.3.17.		
Miscellaneous	56th Divisional Tactical Progress Report No. 6. From 5.0 p.m. 25th March to 5.0 p.m. 26th March, 1917.	27/03/1917	27/03/1917
Miscellaneous	56th Divisional Tactical Progress Report No. 7. From 5.0 p.m. 26th March to 5.0 p.m. 27th March, 1917.	28/03/1917	28/03/1917
Miscellaneous	56th Divisional Tactical Progress Report No. 8. From 5.0 p.m. 27th March to 5.0 p.m. 28th March 1917.	29/03/1917	29/03/1917
Miscellaneous	56th Divisional Tactical Progress Report No. 9. From 5. p.m. 28th March to 5 p.m. 29th March 1917.	30/03/1917	30/03/1917
Miscellaneous	56th Divisional Tactical Progress Report No. 10. from 5 p.m. 29th March to 5 p.m. 30th March 1917.	31/03/1917	31/03/1917
Miscellaneous	56th Divisional Tactical Progress Report No. 11. from 5 p.m. 30th March to 5 p.m. 31st March, 1917.	01/04/1917	01/04/1917
Miscellaneous	56th Divn. G.A.75.	27/03/1917	27/03/1917
Miscellaneous	56th Division Instructions. Medical Arrangements	28/03/1917	28/03/1917
Miscellaneous	56th Division Instructions. Action Of Massed Machine Guns.	29/03/1917	29/03/1917
Miscellaneous	56th Division Instructions. Assembly Areas & Allotment Of Trenches For Traffic.	30/03/1917	30/03/1917
Map	Secret		
Miscellaneous	56th Div. G.A.100.	30/03/1917	30/03/1917
Miscellaneous	56th Division Instructions. Maps.	31/03/1917	31/03/1917
Miscellaneous	56th Division Instructions. Employment of R.E. & Pioneers.	31/03/1917	31/03/1917
Miscellaneous	56th Divisions Instructions Arrangements For Liaison With Neighbouring Units.	31/03/1917	31/03/1917
Miscellaneous	56th Division Instructions. Concentration.	31/03/1917	31/03/1917
Map	Concentration Z-1		
Miscellaneous	56th Division Instructions. Operations.	31/03/1917	31/03/1917
Miscellaneous	Offensive Operations On VII Corps Front. 56th Divisional Instructions No. 1. Appendix D	13/03/1917	13/03/1917
Map			
Map	Reference Brigade HQ		
Miscellaneous	56th Divn. G.434. Appendix E	08/03/1917	08/03/1917
Miscellaneous	A Form. Messages And Signals.		
Miscellaneous	Instructions Regarding Rations During The Forthcoming Operations.	26/03/1917	26/03/1917

Miscellaneous	Situation Of Dumped Rations On Z Day.		
Miscellaneous			
Miscellaneous	Administrative Instructions (1) For Offensive Operations.	30/03/1917	30/03/1917
Miscellaneous	Contents Of Ammunition & Water Dumps.		
Miscellaneous	Situation Of Dumped Rations On Z Day.		
Heading	File 'D' Offensive Operations On VII Corps Front Operation Order From Neighbouring Divisions. 1917 May		
Operation(al) Order(s)	30th Division Operation Order No. 59.	18/03/1917	18/03/1917
Operation(al) Order(s)	14th Division Operation Order No. 108.	18/03/1917	18/03/1917
Heading	File B.2. Offensive Operation On VII Corps Front Correspondence From Brigades To 1917 Mar		
Miscellaneous	Headquarters, 56th Division.	18/03/1917	18/03/1917
Miscellaneous	Report On German Wire Entanglements H.1 Sector.	17/03/1917	17/03/1917
Miscellaneous	Report On British Wire Entanglements H.1 Sector.	17/03/1917	17/03/1917
Miscellaneous	168th. Infantry Brigade	16/03/1917	16/03/1917
Map	Map B		
Map	Map A		
Map	Map C		
Map	Map D		
Miscellaneous	Headquarters. 56th. Division.	16/03/1917	16/03/1917
Heading	File A.2. Offensive Operations On VII Corps Front Correspondence With Corps.		
Miscellaneous	56th Division No. GA 41	18/03/1917	18/03/1917
Miscellaneous		16/03/1917	16/03/1917
Miscellaneous	C Form Messages And Signals.		
Miscellaneous	56th Division G.A.10.	14/03/1917	14/03/1917
Map			
Miscellaneous	56th Division No GA.11.	14/03/1917	14/03/1917
Miscellaneous	56th Divn. No GA.9.	14/03/1917	14/03/1917
Miscellaneous	Reference proposed scheme for an indirect Machine Gun Barrage on the Corps front to assist the advance of the Infantry and General Hull's remarks	16/03/1917	16/03/1917
Miscellaneous	General Holls Remarks		
Miscellaneous	C Form (Duplicate). Messages And Signals.		
Miscellaneous	14th Division.	13/03/1917	13/03/1917
Map	Arras		
Map	Right Div.		

Index

SUBJECT.

Vol 14

No.	Contents.	Date.
	56th Divn: G.S. March '17	

Confidential

War Diary
of
General Staff
Hd Qrs. 56th Division

From 1st March 1917
To   31st March 1917

Army Form C. 2118.

WAR DIARY
or
INTELLIGENCE SUMMARY.
(Erase heading not required.)

Instructions regarding War Diaries and Intelligence Summaries are contained in F. S. Regs., Part II. and the Staff Manual respectively. Title pages will be prepared in manuscript.

Place	Date	Hour	Summary of Events and Information	Remarks and references to Appendices
LAGORGUE	1st March		Visibility was excellent throughout the day, and artillery on both sides was fairly active. During the day 169 Bde were relieved by 146 Bde in the left section.	
	2nd March		Reciprocal artillery activity during the day. Our patrols were active and entered the enemy line.	
	3rd March		A quiet day as visibility was poor. O.O. 70 issued giving orders for 168 Bde. to move by rail.	APPENDIX A
	4th March		Another quiet day, although visibility had improved.	
	5th March		148 Bde. relieved 167 Bde. in the NEUVE CHAPELLE section. 168 Bde HQ moved to CENSE de RAUX. 5th Pioline Regt. entrained for ARRAS.	
WILLEMAN	6th March		Div H.Q. moved to WILLEMAN. III Army O.O. received with orders for division to move into VII Corps. O.O. No 71 received. Div handed over to 49 Div. 6pm.	APPENDIX A
	7th March		G.O.C. + G.S.O.1 arrived at WILLEMAN - Bde. continued marches to new area. Appreciation of GHQ with draft orders by Gen. received from III Corps Commander.	Appendix B
LE CAUROY	8th March		Div HQ moved to LE CAUROY. G.O.C. +5.S.O.1 visited VII Corps. File A. No 6 received.	Appendix C
	9th March		VII Corps opinion roughly outline of offensive operations to be undertaken. O.O. No 72 issued	Appendix
	10th March		G.O.C. + G.S.O.1 visited 14th Divl HQ. Papers referring to offensive received from 46th Divl. G.S.O.1 + G.S.O.2 made reconnaissance of ground actn.	

WAR DIARY
or
INTELLIGENCE SUMMARY

Army Form C. 2118.

Place	Date	Hour	Summary of Events and Information	Remarks and references to Appendices
LECAUROY	11th March		Divisional conference at Div HQ. Brig Genl Cmdg Bdes, ADS Majors, CRA & CRE were present — XI Corps O.O. received to take over the centre sector — the line and O.O. No. 73 issued. G.S.O.1 + G.S.O.2 reconnoitred the divisional sector.	APPENDIX A
	12th March		Readjustment of trench areas.	
	13th March		General instructions reference offensive operations issued.	APPENDIX D
	14th March		During the evening 169 Bde took over the "C" centre sector from 14th and 30th Divisions. 2 81st Bde R.F.A. completed movement into the line.	APPENDIX G
	15th March		10am 56 Div. took over command of the centre sector. A quiet day on the divisional front. Movement into supporting billets completed.	
	16th March		Rather quiet day.	
	17th March		Slight hostile shelling. A number of fires were visible in enemy's line far to the South. Between 1 and 4 am several large explosions were heard in BEAURAINS. Our patrols found the enemy very much on the alert in his trenches.	
	18th Mar			

Army Form C. 2118.

WAR DIARY
or
INTELLIGENCE SUMMARY
(Erase heading not required.)

Instructions regarding War Diaries and Intelligence Summaries are contained in F.S. Regs., Part II. and the Staff Manual respectively. Title Pages will be prepared in manuscript.

Place	Date	Hour	Summary of Events and Information	Remarks and references to Appendices
	19th	p.m. 1.0	VII Corps O.O.78 received.	
		2.10	169th Brigade order line M.23.b.2.4. - M.23.b.30.62. - GRUNDHERR ST. - MANOIR to M.18.c.7.4. SWITCH TR. to M.18 central to be occupied and posts to be pushed out along bank M.24.a.5.1. M.24.b.1.7.	
		5.15	Situation the same, except that 30th Division now hold BEAURAINS - MERCATEL Road from M.23.b.1.2. to S.12.b.9.7.	
		8.15	VII Corps O.O.79 received that no further advance was to be made for the present.	
		9.0	169th Brigade report hostile artillery fairly active from N.E. 2 prisoners of 102 R.I.R. taken at M.24.b.95.65.	
	20th	a.m. 5.30	Slight shelling during night. Patrols report PREUSSEN Redoubt clear to M.12.d.6.2. NEUFCHATEL LANE patrolled to wire round NEUVILLE VITASSE, where enemy were encountered.	
		9.30	169th Brigade report that dispositions ordered in orders issued 2.10 p.m. 19th were now complete A quiet day. and consolidation carried out without interference from enemy.	
		10.0	VII Corps appreciation of situation received and instructions to prepare to assault the COJEUL SWITCH NEUVILLE VITASSE Line. Verbal information of this sent immediately to 169th Brigade.	
		p.m. 5.0	5 Batteries, 56th D.A. now in action in new positions. A quiet day. 56th Divisional Instructions based on Corps appreciation issued.	Appendix D
	21st	a.m. 5.30	A party of Q.W.R. sent out to establish S.P. at M.18.d.7.8. at M.18.b.4.5. and M.18.d.7.8. found strong enemy W.P. at M.18.d.6.8. and were forced to withdraw.	
		9.0	169th Brigade report posts established at M.18.b.4.5. and M.18.d.7.8. and enemy occupying NEUVILLE VITASSE. 169th Brigade issued orders for a forward line to be dug in, parallel to enemy position.	

2449 Wt. W14957/M90 750,000 1/16 J.B.C. & A. Forms/C.2118/12

Army Form C. 2118.

WAR DIARY
or
INTELLIGENCE SUMMARY

(Erase heading not required.)

Instructions regarding War Diaries and Intelligence Summaries are contained in F.S. Regs., Part II. and the Staff Manual respectively. Title Pages will be prepared in manuscript.

Place	Date	Hour	Summary of Events and Information	Remarks and references to Appendices
	21st	p.m. 5.0	Slight shelling during the day of BEAURAINS & ACHICOURT. Our new front line was registered.	
		8.0	VIIth Corps O.O.81 received ordering troops to be closed up and LE CAUROY area evacuated.	
	22nd	a.m. 5.0	There was intermittent shelling of BEAURAINS during the night.	
		p.m 1.0	169th Brigade H.Qrs. moved to ACHICOURT MILL.	
		3.15	Orders were issued for 167th and 168th Brigades, who were still carrying out training in the IVERGNY and SUS-ST.-LEGER Area to move up into the Div.Area.	Appendix A
		11.30 a.m.	56th Div. Warning Order issued No. 77, giving preliminary programme for attack on NEUVILLE VITASSE and the COJEUL SWITCH.	Appendix A
	23rd	5.0	A quieter night although cross roads W. of BEAURAINS were persistently shelled. Work commenced on new line in M.18.b. & d. and good progress made.	
			Evening Report. Our new trench was registered with 4.2" Hows. & 77 mm. guns and BEAURAINS was shelled during the day.	
		p.m. 8.0	VII Corps O.O.82 received saying that 50th Div. Arty. would on arrival be grouped under 56th Div. Arty.	
	24th	a.m. 5.0	There was some shelling of the posts established in PREUSSEN Redoubt and the new line and some M.G.activity.	
			Evening Report - A quiet day. There was a noticeable absence of sniping from TELEGRAPH HILL Brigadier-Generals Commanding 167th and 168th Brigades, G.S.O.1 and A.A.Q.M.G. at a Conference with Divisional Commander at Div. H.Q.	
	25th	a.m. 5.0	Hostile field guns and M.Gs. were active in the early part of the evening. A patrol was fired on at close range by M.G. from about M.24.b.6.2.	
			Inter-battalion relief was carried out in the left sub-section. Evening Report. Hostile artillery was more active in the morning.	

2449 Wt. W14957/M90 750,000 1/16 J.B.C. & A. Forms/C.2118/12.

Army Form C. 2118.

WAR DIARY
or
INTELLIGENCE SUMMARY

(Erase heading not required.)

Instructions regarding War Diaries and Intelligence Summaries are contained in F. S. Regs, Part II. and the Staff Manual respectively. Title Pages will be prepared in manuscript.

Place	Date	Hour	Summary of Events and Information	Remarks and references to Appendices
	26th	a.m. 5.0	Hostile artillery active on front line and BEAURAINS during the night. A party estimated at between 20 and 30 attacked our post at M.18.b.20.85., but were driven off by L.G. and rifle fire. Our casualties - 3 wounded by bombs.	
		p.m. 1.0	VII Corps O.O. No. 83 received laying down the rear line of resistance for the Division as the old German front line system.	
			Evening Report. Enemy field guns active on front line, and the roads in BEAURAINS were shelled during the day. Our guns commenced carrying out wire-cutting programme.	
	27th	5.0 a.m.	VII Corps O.O. No. 85 received saying that 50th Div. Arty. would arrive at WAILLY on the 30th.	
			56th Division G.A.75 issued re move of 50th Div. Arty.	Appendix D
		5.0	Quiet night. Our patrols were active and reported PINE LANE held in strength and large working parties. M.G. fire was opened on another patrol when moving up NEUFCHATEL LANE, 30 yds. forward our front line.	
	28th	a.m 5.0	Evening Report - A quite day. Our guns continued wire-cutting programme.	
			Quiet night. Our patrols were active, and found enemy W.Ps. all along the line engaged in repairing damage done to his wire.	
			Evening Report. Hostile Artillery fairly active during day. Wire-cutting programmes were continued by our artillery.	
		10.0 a.m	56th Div.O.O.No.78 issued with orders for relief of 169th Brigade by 167th and 168th in the line.	Appendix A
	29th	5.0	Enemy Howitzers and M.Gs. active during night. Patrols reported enemy wire being actively repaired and PINE TRENCH and NEUVILLE VITASSE strongly held and garrisons on the alert.	
			Evening Report - quite day. Our artillery was active, carrying out destructive and wire cutting fire on NEUVILLE VITASSE and TELEGRAPH HILL.	

Army Form C. 2118.

WAR DIARY
or
INTELLIGENCE SUMMARY

(Erase heading not required.)

Instructions regarding War Diaries and Intelligence Summaries are contained in F. S. Regs., Part II and the Staff Manual respectively. Title Pages will be prepared in manuscript.

Place	Date	Hour	Summary of Events and Information	Remarks and references to Appendices
	30th	a.m. 5.0	Quite night. Patrols report that gaps in wire have been repaired. Evening Report. Some shelling of our roads and trenches during day. 169 Inf Bde carried out an inter battalion relief. Following instructions issued by 56 Division:- Medical Arrangements - Action of Massed Machine Guns - Assembly areas - Signal Trim - Maps -	APPENDIX "B" Appendix D
	31		Hostile Artillery more active. Much movement and work seen in the course of the day behind the German lines. Following Instructions issued by 56 Division:- Employment of RE and Pioneers - Hosm - Concentration - Operations	Appendix D

T.O. Kidd
Lieut
to Lt. Col. General Staff.

SECRET.   War Diary. Appendix A

COPY NO. 31

56th DIVISION ORDER NO. 70.

3rd March, 1917.

Ref. Sheet 11 LENS   )
Sheet 5A. HAZEBROUCK.) 1:100,000

1. In continuation of 56th Division Order No. 69 dated 25th February, 1917, the 168th Infantry Brigade Group will move to the WILLEMAN No. 1 Area partly by Tactical Train, partly by road.

2. Date of entrainment will be March 10th.

3. Entraining Station will be MERVILLE.

4. Detraining Station will be PETIT HOUVIN.

5. Appendix A gives the units proceeding (a) By Rail (b) By Road.

6. On March 13th the 513th Field Coy. R.E. will march from WILLEMAN No. 1 Area to WILLEMAN No. 3 Area to join 169th Infantry Brigade, and 512th Field Coy. R.E. at present with 169th Infantry Brigade will march to join 168th Infantry Brigade in WILLEMAN No. 1 Area.

7. A map shewing the billeting in the ST. VENANT Area and Accommodation Tables for the PERNES Area is issued with copy No. 32.

8. ACKNOWLEDGE.

H.Q. 56th Division.

Issued at:-

W. Brook Captain
for Lieut.-Colonel.
General Staff.

P.T.O.

Copy No. 1 167th Inf. Bde.
2. 168th Inf. Bde.
3. 169th Inf. Bde.
4. 49th Division.
5. XVIII Corps.
6. XIX Corps.
7. Third Army.
8. 5th Division.
9. 57th Division.
10. C.R.A.
11. C.R.E.
12 & 13. XIth Corps.
14. 1/5th Ches. Regt.
15. A.D.M.S.
16. "Q".
17. A.P.M.
18. 193rd Div. M.G. Coy.
19. Sec. 15th Bty. M.M.G. Coy.
20. 56th Div. Signals.
21. 56th Div. Train.
22. Divl. M. G. Officer.
23. 257th Tunnelling Coy.
24. Divnl. Gas Officer.
25. D.A.D.O.S.
26. 4th Aust. Div. Supply Col.
27. No. 2 Amm. Sub Park.
28. G.O.C.
29. A.D.C.
30. War Diary.
31. File.
32. 513th Field Coy. R.E.

APPENDIX A.

(A) Proceeding By Rail.   (B) By Road.

     Units.   Vehicles.

H.Q. 168th Inf. Bde.   1.L.G.S.   2 G.S. wagons for tools
Signal Section.   1.L.G.S.
168th M.G. Coy.   All.
168th T.M. Bty.   All.
168th Inf. Bde.   (16 Cookers.   8 L.G.S. for S.A.A.
                      (4 Mess Carts.   4 L.G.S. for grenades.
                      (4 Maltese Carts
                      (8 Water Carts.
                      (4 L.G.S. for S.A.A.
                      (8 L.G.S. for tools.
                      (44 Chargers.
                      (36 Pack Ponies.
                      (16 L.G.S. & Hand Carts
                      (for Lewis Guns.

Personnel Heavy   513th Field Coy. R.E.
   T.M. Battery.   No. 3 Coy. Div. Train.
                                            2nd/2nd Field Amb.

Personnel Medium
T.M. Batteries

MARCH TABLE
for
MARCHING PORTION OF 168th INFANTRY BDE. GROUP.

DATE	FROM	TO	ROUTE	REMARKS.
9/10th	Line	LA GORGUE, LESTREM BOUT. DEVILLE VIELLE CHAPELLE		On relief by 147th Bde. Group.
10th	LA GORGUE, LESTREM	ST. VENANT		
11th	ST. VENANT	PERNES	BUSNES and LILLERS	
12th	PERNES	WILLEMAN NO.1 AREA	No restrictions	

The marching portion of the 168th Infantry Brigade will march under the command of Major KINGSFORD Commanding 513th Field Coy. R.E.

War Diary

SECRET.   56th Divn. S.G.431/20.

AMENDMENTS to 56th DIV. ORDER No. 69.
----

1   Para. 14 of 56th Divisional Order No. 69 is cancelled.

        The following is substituted :-

            The Command of the Left Sector of the XI Corps
              Front will pass to the General Officer Commanding
              49th Division at 6 p.m., March 6th.

2.   Divisional Headquarters will open at WILLEMAN at
12 noon, March 6th

3.   ACKNOWLEDGE.

Head Qrs. 56th Divn.   Lieut-Colonel,
3rd March, 1917.   General Staff.

1.   167th Infantry Bde.   19. Sec.15th Bty.M.M.G.Coy.
2.   168th Infantry Bde.   20. 56th Div.Signals.
3.   169th Infantry Bde.   21. 56th Div. Train.
4.   49th Division.   22. Divl. M.G.Officer.
5.   XVIII Corps.   23. 257th Tunnelling Coy.
6.   XIX Corps.   24. Divnl. Gas Officer.
7.   Third Army   25. D.A.D.O.S.
8.   5th Division.   26. 4th Aust.Div.Supply Col.
9.   57th Division.   27. No. 2 Amm.Sub-Park.
10. C.R.A.   28. G.O.C.
11. C.R.E.   29. A.D.C.
12.) XI Corps.   30. War Diary.
13.)   31. File.
14. 1/5th Ches. Regt.
15. A.D.M.S.
16. "Q"
17. A.P.M.
18. 193rd Div. M.G.Coy.

SECRET. *War Diary* Copy No. 25

56th DIVISION ORDER No. 71.

Reference LENS Sheet 11 - 1/100,000.

March 6th 1917.

1. The 56th Division will be transferred to the VII Corps.

2. The Division will march to the VII Corps area in accordance with the attached March Table.

3. Supply Railheads will be :-

   March 8th (less Div. R.A. & 168th Brigade Group) FREVENT.

   " 9th (less Div. R.A. & 168th Bde. Group) BOUQUEMAISON

   " 9th Div. R.A. FREVENT.

   " 10th Division complete BOUQUEMAISON.

4. Accommodation Tables for the FLERS AREA are attached and form Appendix "A".

5. Captain CREIGHTON, 167th Infantry Brigade will reconnoitre the FLERS AREA on the morning of the 7th March, and will rejoin the 167th Infantry Brigade at PERNES the same day.

6. The A.D.M.S. will arrange for the evacuation of C.R 169th Infantry Brigade temporarily unfit, at present in the WILLEMAN No. 2 AREA, to the 169th Brigade Area IVERGNY - SUS.

7. 169th Brigade stores dumped at REGNAUVILLE & WAIL will be conveyed to IVERGNY under arrangements made by S.M.T.O. XIX Corps on March 7th.

8. Divisional Headquarters will close at WILLEMAN and re-open at Le CAUROY on March 8th at an hour to be notified later.

9. ACKNOWLEDGE.

Head Qrs. 56th Divn.

Lieut-Colonel,
General Staff.

Issued at

Copy No. 1.	167th Inf. Bde.	17.	56th Div. Train.
2.	168th Inf. Bde.	18.	Divnl. M.G. Officer
3.	169th Inf. Bde.	19.	Divnl. Gas Officer
4.	XVIII Corps.	20.	D.A.D.O.S.
5.	XIX Corps.	21.	4th Aust. Div. Supply Coy.
6.	Third Army.	22.	No. 2 Amm. Sub Park.
7.	C.R.A.	23.	G.O.C.
8.	C.R.E.	24.	A.D.C.
9 & 10.	XI Corps.	25.	War Diary.
11.	1/5th Ches. Regt.	26.	VII Corps.
12.	A.D.M.S.	27.	Capt. Creighton.
13.	"Q"	28.	File.
14.	A.P.M.		
15.	193rd Div. M.G. Coy.		
16.	56th Div. Signals.		

MARCH TABLE issued with 56th DIV. ORDER No. 71.

Serial No.	Date 1917.	Unit.	From.	To.	Route.	Under orders issued by	Remarks.
1.	7th March.	169th Inf.Bde. Group.	FROHEN No. 2 AREA.	IVERGNY - SUS- ST. LEGER			Orders issued direct by VII Corps to 169th Infantry Brigade.
2.	7th March.	56th Div.(less 168th & 169th Bde.Groups & Arty.)	ST VENANT.	PERNES AREA.	Via BUSNES & LILLERS	No instructions under orders of B.G.C. 167th Inf. Bde. Group.	
3.	8th March.	56th Div.(less 168th & 169th Inf. Bde.Groups & Div. Arty.)	PERNES AREA.	FLERS AREA (less FLERS & ECOIVRES)	No instructions under orders of B.G.C. 167th Inf.Bde.		To be South of the Road PERNES-HEUCHIN by 10.30 a.m. Div. H.Q. direct to Le CAUROY under O.C. Signals.
4.	8th March.	56th Div.Arty. (less personnel Heavy & medium T.M.Batteries)	LIGNY-les-AIRE	ANVIN Arty. Area.		No instructions under C.R.A. 56th Divn.	
5.	9th March.	56th Div.(less 168th & 169th Bde. Groups & Div. Arty.)	FLERS AREA (less FLERS & ECOIVRES)	LE CAUROY AREA.		No instructions under orders of B.G.C. 167th Infantry Brigade.	
6.	9th March.	56th Div.Arty.	ANVIN Arty. AREA.	BOUBERS Arty. Area.		No instructions under orders of C.R.A. 56th Divn.	Take over 18 pdr. guns & 4.5"Hows. left by 49th Divn. To clear ANVIN Area by 11.0 a.m.
7.	10th March.	56th Div.Arty.	BOUBERS AREA.	VII Corps Area.	Detailed orders to follow.		
8.	10th March.	168th Inf.Bde. Gp.plus personnel H.& M. T.Ms.	MERVILLE.	By train to Third Army - detraining Station will be notified later.			
9.	11th March	Marching portion of 168th	ST.VENANT	VALHUON.			
10.	12th March	do. Inf.Bde.Gp.& 56th Div.	VALHUON.	Le.CAUROY Area.			To be clear of VALHUON by 9.0 a.m.

APPENDIX "A"

FLERS AREA.

BRIGADE BILLETING AREAS.

	Officers.	Other Ranks.	Shelter for Horses.
CROIX (Bde. H.Q.)	24	600	100.
BEAUVOIS	8	600	50.
HERNICOURT (excluding BETHONVAL)	25	600	30.
CROISETTE & WIGNACOURT L'ABBAYETTE	39	1200	200
PRONAY	5	150	10.
GAUCHIN	20	1000	100
SIRACOURT	16	400	100
BLANGERMONT (Bde. H.Q.)	17.	660	200
BLANGERVAL	17	660	60
GUINECOURT	4	200	15
HERICOURT	20	800	125
FRAMECOURT	10.	500	25.
PETIT HOUVIN	8	500	40
NUNCQ (Bde. H.Q.)	40	1200	100
HAUTE COTE	12	500	40
SIBIVILLE	32	900	75
SERICOURT	14	300	30
HONVAL	8	350	10

"A" Form.
MESSAGES AND SIGNALS.

TO: War Diary

Sender's Number.	Day of Month.	In reply to Number.	A A A
G.40	7th		

Reference March Table issued with 56th Div. Order
No. 71 aaa Under Serial Nos. 2, 3, 4, 5 & 6 read
for words "no instructions" read "no restrictions"

From
Place 56th Divin
Time

SECRET.   Copy No ....

56th DIVISION ORDER No. 72.

Reference LENS Sheet 11 - 1/100,000

March 8th 1917.

56th Divisional Artillery.
1. Reference 56th Div. Order No. 71 - The Divisional Artillery will march on the 10th instant, from the BOUFERS Artillery Area to LUCHEUX.

2. Route.
    No restrictions - but troops of the 19th Division will be moving NORTH on the BOUQUEMAISON - FREVENT ROAD.

3. The Column will be clear of FREVENT by 2 p.m.

4. 500 yards distance will be maintained between each Battery and between each section and echelon of the Divisional Ammunition Column.

5. **167th Infantry Brigade.**
    On March 9th, the 167th Infantry Brigade Group will billet as under :-

    Brigade H.Qrs.   )
    T.M.Battery.   ) SUS-St.LEGER.
    M.G.Coy.   )
    "A" & "B" Battalions)

    "C" Battalion.   )
    416th Field Coy.R.E.)
    2/1st Field Ambulance.) IVERGNY.
    No. 2 Coy. Div.Train.)

    "D" Battalion   - BEAUDRICOURT.

6. **168th Infantry Brigade.**
    On detrainment on the 10th, the 168th Infantry Brigade Group will be billeted as under :-

    Brigade H.Qrs.   )
    T.M.Battery.   )
    "A" Battalion.   ) IVERGNY.
    No. 3 Coy. Div. Train.)

    "B" & "C" Battalions.)
    2/2nd Field Ambulance.) Le SOUICH.

    "D" Battalion   BREVILLERS.

    513th Field Coy. R.E.   OPPY.

7. ACKNOWLEDGE.

56th Divn.
Head Qrs.

for Lieut-Colonel,
General Staff.

Issued at 6 p.m.

Copies No. 1. 167th Inf.Bde.   No.10. A.P.M.
    to   2. 168th Inf. Bde.   11. 1/5th Ches.Regt.
           3. 169th Inf. Bde.   12. O.C.56th Div.Signals.
           4. "Q"   13. O.C.56th Div. Train.
      5 & 6. VII Corps.   14. Div. M.G.Officer
           7. C.R.A.   15. D.A.D.O.S.
           8. C.R.E.   16. No. 4 Aust.Div.Supply Column.
           9. A.D.M.S.   17. No. 2 Ammunition Sub Park.
                                      18. War Diary
                                      19. A.D.C. for G.O.C.
                                      20 File.

SECRET.   Copy No. 25

56th DIVISION ORDER No. 73.

Reference Map - LENS 51B S.W.1 - 1/100,000.   11th March 1917.

1. 56th Division is to take over the Centre Section of VIIth Corps front (M.10.c.2.2. - M.4.b.3.1.) on March 13th & 14th.

2. 169th Infantry Brigade will take over the above frontage as per Relief Table attached. Relief to be arranged direct between G.O.C., 169th Infantry Brigade and G.O.C's 43rd & 21st Infantry Brigades, and completed on the night 14/15th inst.

3. The responsibility of the 169th Infantry Brigade for defence within its boundaries extends as far back as a N. & S. line through the centre of DAINVILLE.
The boundaries of the Section are as follows :-
Right boundary (with 30th Division.)
M.10.c.2.2. - M.9.b.20.05. - M.9.a.5.6. - thence ACHICOURT - AGNY Railway at M.3.c.5.3. - bridge M.2.d.7.2. - track to M.2.c.9.4. - M.2.c.7.2. - thence GOWER ST. (inclusive).

Left boundary (with 14th Division)
M.4.b.3.1. - support line at M.4.a.98.30 - Reserve line at M.4.a.50.85. - G.33.d.95.40 - thence HAVANNAH ST. (inclusive)

Sketch Map showing Divisional boundaries is also attached.

4. At 8 p.m. 14th inst., 30th Division will take over from 169th Infantry Brigade its responsibility as regards supporting 58th Division in case of emergency.

5. One battalion of 167th Infantry Brigade will move to DAINVILLE on 14th inst., as per March Table attached, where it will be at the disposal of A.D. Signals, VIIth Corps, for burying cable.
The name of the Unit detailed to be reported to Div.H.Q. by 12th inst.

6. 56th Div. Artillery will move into the line under detailed instructions to be issued by G.O.C., R.A., VIIth Corps.

7. 513th Field Coy, R.E. will be attached to 169th Infantry Brigade and will move up as per March Table attached.

8. The relief of the Field Ambulance, 14th Division, will be carried out under arrangements to be made by the A.D.M.S.

9. "L" Special Coy. R.E. and 2 Sections 181st Tunnelling Coy. R.E. now attached to 30th Division will be attached to 56th Division from March 14th.

10. Progress and completion of reliefs to be reported to Div. H.Q.

11. G.O.C., 56th Division will assume command of the line at 10 a.m. 15th inst.

12. ACKNOWLEDGE.

B. Pakenham
Lieut-Colonel,
General Staff.

Head Qrs. 56th Divn.

Issued at 9-15 p.m.

P.T.O.

Copy No. 1. 167th Inf.Bde.	15. 193rd Div.M.G.Coy.
2. 168th Inf.Bde.	16. 56th Div.Signals.
3. 169th Inf.Bde.	17. 56th Div. Train.
4. 14th Division.	18. Divnl. M.G.Officer.
5. 30th Division.	19. Divnl. Gas Officer.
6 & 7. VIIth Corps.	20. D.A.D.O.S.
8. 21st Division.	21. 4th Aust.Div.SupplyCol.
9. C.R.A.	22. No. 2 Amm.Sub Park.
10. C.R.E.	23. G.O.C.
11. 1/5th Cheshire Regt.	24. A.D.C.
12. A.D.M.S.	25. War Diary.
13. "Q"	26. File.
14. A.P.M.	

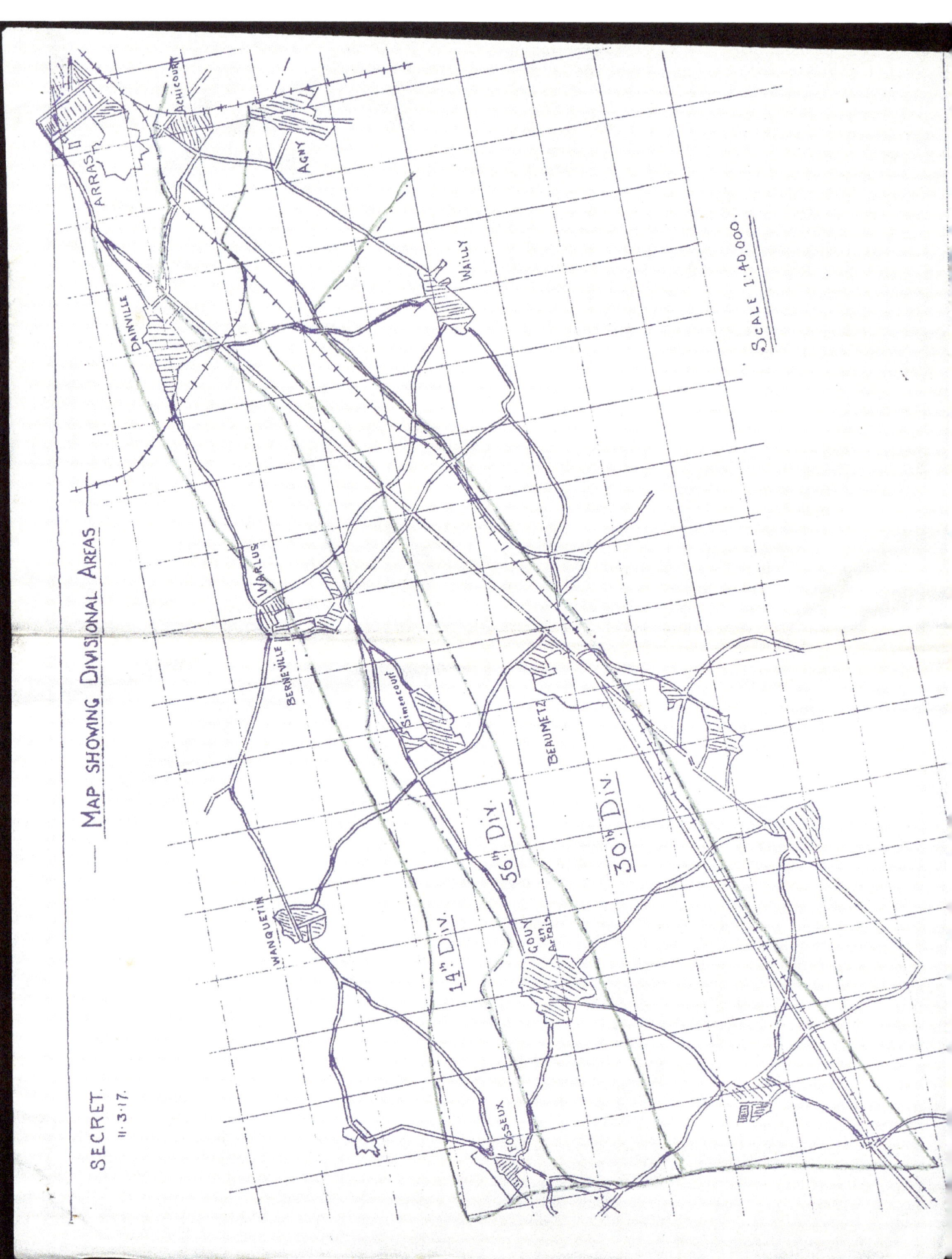

RELIEF & MARCH TABLE attached to 56th DIV. ORDER No.73, dated March 11th 1917.

Unit.	Date 1917.	From.	To.	Route.	Remarks.
169th Brigade.					
"A" Battalion.	March 13/14th.	Present Brigade Area.	ACHICOURT.	Troops will march by the main ARRAS – DOULLENS RD. (2). No troops are to use the GOUY-en-ARTOIS – BAC de SUD ROAD or the main ARRAS – DOULLENS ROAD between the BAC de SUD & ARRAS before 6 p.m. (3). 100 yds. interval between Companies will be maintained.	In relief of "A" Battalion – 21st Inf. Brigade, 30th Division.
169th M.G.Coy.	" "	do.	ACHICOURT.		
169th T.M.Bty.	" "	do.	ACHICOURT.		
169th Bde. H.Q.	March 14/15th	Present Brigade Area.	DAINVILLE.		To take over Brigade H.Qrs. of 21st Brigade.
"A" Battn.	" "	ACHICOURT	LINE.		In relief of "A" Battn. 43rd L.I.Brigade.
169th M.G.Coy.	" "	ACHICOURT.	LINE.		
169th T.M.Bty.	" "	ACHICOURT.	LINE.		
"B" Battn.	" "	Present Brigade Area.	ACHICOURT.		In relief of "A" Battn. 169th Brigade.
"C" & "D" Battalions.	" "	Present Brigade Area.	ARRAS		In relief of 2 Battns. 43rd L.I.Brigade.
513th Fl.Coy. R.E.	" "	do.	ACHICOURT.		
167th Brigade "A" Battn.	March 15/16th.	Present Brigade Area.	DAINVILLE.		To bury cable under orders of A.D.Corps Signals from the 16th March onwards.

SECRET.

AMENDMENT to 56th DIV. ORDER No. 73

On night of 14/15th "D" Battalion 169th Infantry Brigade will be billeted in DAINVILLE and not ARRAS.
In DAINVILLE this Battalion will relieve "A" Battalion 42nd L.I.Brigade.

2. On the night of the 15/16th "D" Battalion, 169th Infantry Brigade will move into ARRAS in relief of "A" Battalion, 43rd L.I.Brigade.

3. On the night of the 15/16th "A" Battalion, 167th Infantry Brigade will march to DAINVILLE in relief of "D" Battalion, 169th Infantry Brigade.
This battalion will be attached to 169th Infantry Brigade on its arrival in DAINVILLE, but will be at the disposal of A.D. Signals, VIIth Corps for work. G.O.C. 169th Infantry Brigade will have a call upon this battalion in case of attack.

4. "A" Battalion, 169th Infantry Brigade, billeted in ACHICOURT on the night 13/14th inst., will be at the disposal of G.O.C., 21st Infantry Brigade in case of emergency, until such time as the latter is relieved by 89th Infantry Brigade on 14th inst. (timed for 1 p.m.)

B Pakenham
Lieut-Colonel,
General Staff.

Head Qrs. 56th Divn.
12th March, 1917.

No.		No.	
1.	167th Inf. Bde.	15.	193rd Div. M.G.Coy.
2.	168th Inf. Bde.	16.	56th Div. Signals.
3.	169th Inf. Bde.	17.	56th Div. Train.
4.	14th Division.	18.	Divnl. M.G.Officer.
5.	30th Division.	19.	Divnl. Gas Officer.
6 & 7.	VIIth Corps.	20.	D.A.D.O.S.
8.	21st Division.	21.	4th Aust.Div.Supply Column.
9.	C.R.A.	22.	No. 2 Amm.Sub. Park.
10.	C.R.E.	23.	G.O.C.
11.	1/5th Cheshire Regt.	24.	A.D.C.
12.	A.D.M.S.	25.	War Diary.
13.	"Q"	26.	File.
14.	A.P.M.		

"A" Form.
MESSAGES AND SIGNALS.

Army Form C. 212

TO: WAR DIARY

Sender's Number: G.69
Day of Month: 12th

AAA

Reference 56th Division Order No. 73 of 11th March 1917 AAA Paragraph 8 for 14th Division read 30th Division

Sent to all recipients of OO.73

From: 56th Division
Time: 10 15a

SECRET.   Copy No. 24

56th DIVISION ORDER No. 74.

18th March 1917.

1. (a). The enemy has begun his withdrawal opposite our front and the leading troops of VII Corps have now crossed into the enemy trenches.

   (b). The 30th Division has occupied M.26.b.4.6. - M.21.c.1.1. - M.21.c.5.1. and MARLBOROUGH TRENCH.

   (c). 169th Infantry Brigade has occupied BEAURAINS.

   (d). 14th Division are in KRIEGER STELLUNG and has sent patrols over the ridge S.E. of that trench.

   (e). It is probable that the enemy will now withdraw quickly to his main defensive line - TELEGRAPH HILL - COJEUL SWITCH - Eastern half of NEUVILLE VITASSE.

2. 169th Infantry Brigade will keep close touch with the enemy on its front and occupy the ground as he vacates it.

   This advance will be carried out cautiously, and G.O.C. 169th Infantry Brigade will avoid becoming involved in a serious engagement at present. Close touch must be maintained with 30th Division on the right and 14th Division on the Left.

3. The map attached shews :-

   (a). Boundaries between Divisions in the forward move - in Green.

   (b). The first objective to be secured in Black. This line is to be firmly consolidated.

   (c). Further objectives to be secured as opportunities offer - in Blue.

   (d). The Blue dotted line shows the next further objective to be secured.

4. The forward movement will probably develop from the right and will be taken up by Divisions in succession from the right.

5. 56th Divisional Artillery has been placed at the disposal of the Division.

   The C.R.A. will reconnoitre for forward positions & be prepared to move forward batteries as the situation developes.

6. The 1/7th Middlesex Regiment is placed at the disposal of G.O.C., 169th Infantry Brigade.

7. 167th Infantry Brigade (less 1/7th Middlesex Regiment) & 168th Infantry Brigade will continue training. 167th Inf. Brigade will be kept at 7 hours notice.

8. The 1/5th Cheshire Regiment (Pioneers) are placed at the disposal of the C.R.E. for improving communications to allow of artillery, etc. moving forward

/9.

P.T.O.

2.

9. The A.D.M.S. will make the necessary medical arrangements.

10. Div. H.Q. will move to-morrow to BEAUMETZ-les-LOGES at an hour to be notified later.

11. ACKNOWLEDGE by WIRE.

B Pakenham
Lieut-Colonel,
General Staff.

Head Qrs. 56th Divn.

Issued at 5.30 p.m. 18.3.17.

Copy No.			
1.	167th Infantry Brigade	14.	193rd Div.M.G.Coy.
2.	168th Infantry Brigade	15.	56th Div. Signals.
3.	169th Infantry Brigade	* 16.	56th Div. Train.
4.	30th Division.	17.	Div. M.G.Officer.
5.	14th Division.	* 18.	Div. Gas Officer.
6.&	VII Corps	* 19.	D.A.D.O.S.
7.		* 20.	4th Aust.Div.Supply Column
8.	C.R.A.	* 21.	No. 2 Ammn.Sub Park.
9.	C.R.E.	22.	G.O.C.
10.	1/5th Ches. Regt.	* 23.	A.D.C.
11.	A.D.M.S.	24.	War Diary.
12.	"Q"	25.	File.
13.	A.P.M.	26.	21st Division.

* Map not attached.

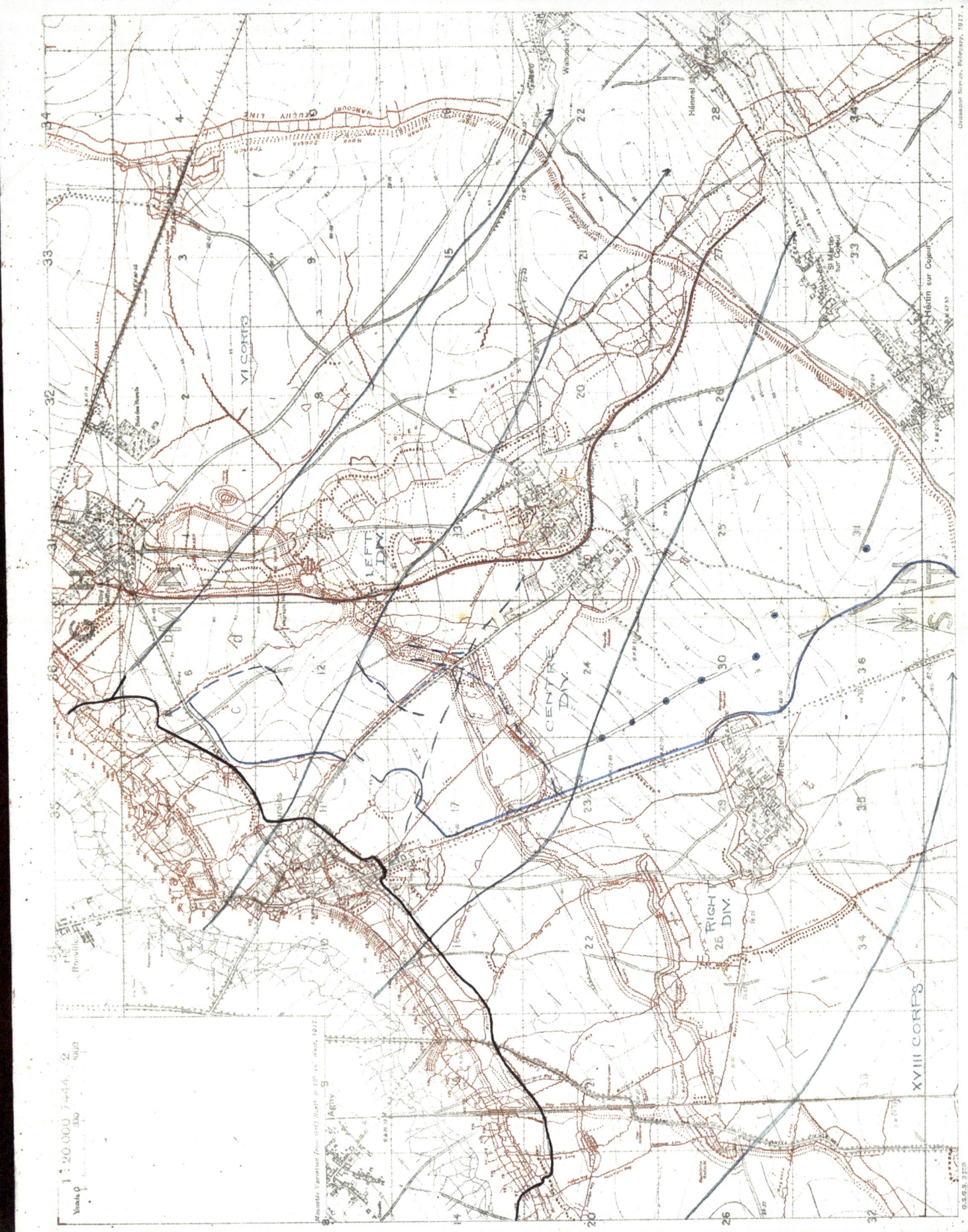

War Diary

SECRET.

Copy No 24

56th DIVISIONAL ORDER No. 75.

18th March 1917.

1. 169th Infantry Brigade will not endeavour to gain more ground to the front until the line which has now been reached has been made quite secure.

    Strong points must be made and if possible connected; ammunition, stores and water must be brought forward, signal communication established and patrols sent forward as already ordered.

2. The C.R.A. will arrange that artillery support is ensured.

3. If the enemy is found at daylight to have withdrawn still further, the 169th Infantry Brigade will methodically resume the advance in conformity with the movements of the Brigades on its right and left.

4. Any inclination of the leading troops to press forward to insecure positions in close proximity to the enemy's main defensive line must be checked.

5. The Blue Line on the map issued with 56th Divisional Order No. 74 of 18.3.17 indicates approximately the limit of the general advance. Positions in advance of the Blue Line must be gradually built up.

6. ACKNOWLEDGE.

B. Pakenham
Lieut-Colonel,
General Staff.

Head Qrs. 56th Divn.

Issued at 10.45 p.m

Copy No. 1. 167th Infantry Brigade
2. 168th Infantry Brigade.
3. 169th Infantry Brigade.
4. 30th Division.
5. 14th Division.
6 & 7. VII Corps.
8. C.R.A.
9. C.R.E.
10. 1/5th Ches. Regt.
11. A.D.M.S.
12. "Q"
13. A.P.M.
14. 193rd Div. M.G.Coy.
15. 56th Div. Signals.
16. 56th Div. Train.
17. Div. M.G.Officer.
18. Div. Gas Officer.
19. D.A.D.O.S.
20. 4th Aust.Div.Supply Col.
21. No.2 Ammn.Sub Park.
22. G.O.C.
23. A.D.C.
24. War Diary.
25. File.
26. 21st Division.

SECRET. Copy No. 20

56th DIVISIONAL ORDER No.76.

22nd March 1917.

Moves will take place to-morrow (23rd) as per attached March Table.

ACKNOWLEDGE.

Head Qrs. 56th Divn.

Lieut-Colonel,
General Staff.

Issued at 3.15 pm

Copy No. 1. 167th Infantry Brigade.
2. 168th Infantry Brigade.
3. 169th Infantry Brigade.
4. C.R.A.
5. C.R.E.
6. 1/5th Cheshire Regt.
7. A.D.M.S.
8. "Q"
9. A.P.M.
10. 193rd Div. M.G.Coy.
11. 56th Div. Signals.
12. 56th Div. Train.
13. Div. M.G.Officer.
14. Div. Gas Officer.
15. D.A.D.O.S.
16. 4th Aust. Div. Supply Column.
17. No. 2 Ammn. Sub Park.
18. G.O.C.
19. A.D.C.
20. War Diary.
21. File.
22. 7th Corps.
23. Town Major, GOUY-on-ARTOIS
24. Town Major, BOLCHIET
25. Town Major, BEAUMETZ-en-LOGES.
26. Town Major, AGNY.

MARCH TABLE ISSUED WITH 56th DIVISION ORDER NO. 76.

UNIT.	DATE.	FROM.	TO.	ROUTE.	REMARKS.
167th Brigade Group (less 1 Battn.)	March 23rd	Present Area	MOLCHIET	WARLUZEL-SAULTY-BAVINCOURT.	Note to enter BAVINCOURT before 1 p.m. 500 yards interval between units.
No. 2 Coy. Train	"	-do-	BAVINCOURT		Under orders of Brigadier-General Commanding 167th Bde.
7th Middlesex Regt.	"	-do-	AGNY		Orders given direct to O.C. 7th Middlesex Regiment.
168th Brigade Group (less one Battn and No 3 Coy Train)	23rd March	Present Area	GOUY-on-ARTOIS	SOMBRIN-BARLY	Not to enter SOMBRIN 11.a.m., to be clear of BARLY by 2.p.m. 500 yards interval between units.
1 Battalion 168th Brigade.	-do-	-do-	BEAUMETZ	-do-	Under orders of Brigadier General Commanding 168th Brigade.
No 3 Coy. Train.	"	-do-	BAVINCOURT.	-do-	

Orders for move of Field Companies have been issued by C.R.E.

SECRET.   56th Division. G.A.43.

169th Infantry Brigade.)
167th Infantry Brigade.)
168th Infantry Brigade.)
C.R.A.   )
C.R.E.   )   For information.
30th Division.   )
14th Division.   )

      With a view to a resumption of the operations at an early date, preparations must be begun at once, with a view to allowing of the assembly of assaulting troops, and of their being able to start square with their objective.

      The task of the Division is given in 56th Division No. G.A.43 ("Appreciation and Instructions") which is circulated herewith.

      The General Officer Commanding 169th Infantry Brigade, will, therefore, carry out the following:-

(1) Construct strong points in PREUSSEN WORK about where the 3 trenches are cut by the tramline, viz:- M.18.b.24 - M.18.b.36 - M.18.b.2.9.

(2) Construct a strong point in NEUVILLE LANE about M.24.b.53.

(3) Construct a strong point in VITASSE LANE about M.24.b.57.

(4) Construct strong point about M.18.d.78.

(5) Reclaim DEODAR LANE between M.18.d.63 to M.18.b.75.20 and connect with PREUSSEN WORK about its junction with the railway M.18.b.4.4.

(6) Dig trench in continuation of DEODAR LANE, connecting up strong points in (2) and (3) above, and going as far south as M.24. Central where junction should be made with 30th Division. This trench must be well traversed, in view of enfilade fire from the north.

      The progress of the above work will be reported.

      ACKNOWLEDGE.

(Sd.) E. PACKENHAM.
Lieut.-Colonel.
General Staff.

H.Q. 56th Division.
20th March, 1917.

1. Brickfields.
2. Stone built, solid Chateau.
3. Very solid stone house.
4. Solid stone farm, with outhouses of brick, 18in. thick.
5. Big stone house.
6. Watering place.
7. Large solid brick and stone house.
8. Chateau and farm, former brick, latter stone, very strong.
9. Sugar factory, of brick, very solid.
10. Mairie, stone, very solid.
11. Watering place.
12. Big Chateau, with stables, outhouses, brick and stone, very strong.
13. Big stone built farm.
14. Large solid house, of stone.
15. Stone and brick Chateau.
16. Distillery, of brick, solid.
17. Chateau, brick, solid.
18. Big, solid, brick house.
19. Ditto.
20. Old windmill, with walls 2.35m. thick, very strong.
21. Church, with tower, strongly built.
22. Farm, large, of brick and stone, walls standing.
23. Farm, of brick, standing.
24. Brick building, solid.
25. Ditto.

WELLS.—Nearly every house has one (windlass) in its yard or just outside. Average depth 35m.

UNDERGROUND PASSAGES.—Deep and wide under house and grounds of pt. 12. Reported wide enough for cart and horse to drive along. Another reported connecting pts. 7 and 12.

NEUVILLE VITASSE

3rd Field Survey Coy R.E. (1290).

Scale 1:5000.

Trenches Corrected to 6.3.17.

REFERENCE.
- Buildings roofed and apparently complete.
- Buildings partly or wholly demolished.
- △ Dumps.
- O.P's.
- Trench Mortars.
- Good Cellars or Dug-outs.
- M.G. Emplacements.

SECRET.   56th Divn. G.A.43.

                                                   Copy No.......

VII CORPS APPRECIATION and INSTRUCTIONS.

Recent events necessitate a considerable modification of the VII Corps plans.

The enemy's main defensive line now runs as shown by the Red Line on the attached map, continuing south eastwards along the COJEUL SWITCH.   He has now withdrawn to that line, and the indications are that he proposes to stand there.

Assuming that this is so, his withdrawal has had no effect on the Third Army plan for attack, except that the new line instead of the old becomes the first objective of the VII Corps.

2.   It is clearly impracticable for us, in the time at our disposal, to mount a frontal assault against the German line running from NEUVILLE VITASSE   south eastwards. The task of the Corps therefore resolves itself into holding the enemy on this latter portion of his line, and preparing to attack from the West on the front from NEUVILLE VITASSE to the HARP in conjunction with the main attack of the VI and XVII Corps.

3.   The initial assault will therefore be delivered by two Divisions only - the 14th on the left against TELEGRAPH HILL and the southern part of the HARP, and the 56th Division on the right against NEUVILLE VITASSE.   The assault will be delivered at Zero + 2 hours, as the Corps on our left have to take their Black line first.

The zones of attack allotted to these two Divisions are shown between the green dividing lines.

The first objective is shown in Blue.   There will be a pause of 4 hours on this objective in order to conform to the VI Corps plan; and during this pause the 30th Division on the right will move up to the Blue line as shown in their zone.

The second objectives are shown in Brown.   The 30th Division will advance in line with the other two from the Blue line, which will be left at Zero + 6 hours 40 minutes.

The 30th Division will probably be able to push straight on and seize the high ground at N.34. and 35. and T.4. and 5. assisted by the 58th Division, which will be holding the front between the SENSEE and COJEUL Rivers.

4.   The Heavy Artillery about DAINVILLE and S.W. of it will have to be brought forward to positions in and between the CRINCHON and COJEUL Valleys.   Some assistance can be expected from the Artillery of the Fifth Army on our right.

The artillery plan will be framed with the following objects :-

(a). Cutting the wire along the front of assault; this will probably have to be done by the guns and Howitzers, as it will not be possible to get Medium Trench Mortars up within wire cutting range.

(b). Demolishing the works in NEUVILLE VITASSE, on TELEGRAPH HILL, and in the HARP.

(c). Counter battery work.

(d). The usual barrages for the assault.

5.   The probable task of the Reserve Division (21st) is for future consideration.

/6.

6. The above general plan is issued in order to guide Divisions and the Corps Artillery in their preparations, which must be pushed on with at once. There is very little time.

As many troops as possible must be kept back at training.

The conditions are unstable and plans may change. But in the meantime the lines indicated in these instructions are those along which Divisions will concentrate their energies.

Divisions in arranging their schemes of preparation will give strict priority to the bare essentials; the work must be so arranged that, should an assault be ordered at any time at short notice, the fullest value will be obtained from the work that has been done

It is essential that a minimum state of readiness should be reached as soon as possible.

7. A Map showing the reallotment of areas to Divisions will be issued shortly.

19th March, 1917.

(Sgd.) J. BURNETT STUART,
Brigadier-General,
General Staff, VII Corps.

Issued to :-

167th Inf. Bde.	copy No. 1.
168th Inf. Bde.	No. 2
169th Inf. Bde.	No. 3.
C.R.A.	No. 4.
C.R.E.	No. 5.
"Q"	No. 6.
A.D.M.S.	No. 7.
Div. M.G. Officer	No. 8.
Div. M.G. Coy.	No. 9.
File.	No. 10.

SECRET.   56th Divn. No.G.A.85.

56th DIVISION INSTRUCTIONS.

ACTION OF MASSED MACHINE GUNS.

1. **169th Bde. M.G.Coy.**

    Will provide 8 guns to be placed near M.23.b.7.6. under the orders of the Divisional M.G.Officer.

    <u>Objective.</u> - to fire on the hostile positions from TELEGRAPH WORK in N.7.a. down the COJEUL SWITCH to N.14.c. and also on NEUVILLE VITASSE, covering the advance of the infantry by overhead fire.

    On the occupation of the BLUE LINE by us, these guns will advance to a position in M.24.d. (about the 90 contour line) and assist the attack on the BROWN LINE.

    <u>Ammunition Dumps.</u> - will be formed at M.23.b.7.6.

    <u>Remainder of Company</u> will be with 169th Infantry Brigade in Divisional Reserve.

2. **193rd (Div.) M.G.Coy.**

    Will provide 8 guns, which will be echelonned by the Divisional M.G.Officer as follows :-

    (a) 2 guns about M.11.d.5.9.

    (b) 2 guns in BATTERY TRENCH about M.12.c.85.10.

    (c) 4 guns to assemble as far forward as possible, and, as soon as the attack on the BLUE LINE has been launched, to select positions on the left flank from which to bring fire to bear in a Northerly or North Easterly direction.

    <u>Object.</u> To prevent attacks from the North or North East, and in the event of non-success by the Division on our left, to aid in the formation of a defensive flank by means of cross fire.

    <u>Ammunition Dumps.</u> - near positions (a) & (b) & the site selected for (c).

    <u>Remainder of Company.</u> - will be in Divisional Reserve, with its

    pack

P.T.O.

pack animals, and be ready to move forward quickly as may be required.

3. Co-operation with 30th Division.

30th Division is prepared to provide 8 machine guns about M.30 central to fire into NEUVILLE VITASSE and along the valley South of it until Zero + 2 hours, with the object of keeping the enemy below ground, of preventing reinforcements entering the Village from the S.E., and of causing loss on any enemy driven from the Village.

When the 30th Division has occupied the BLUE LINE these guns are to fire down the valley towards N.20.d. until masked by their own infantry, when they are to be brought into positions which will afford protection to the right flank of 56th Division.

56th Division.

When the capture of NEUVILLE VITASSE has been effected, the Divisional M.G.Officer will arrange to bring forward 8 guns to a position about the N.E. end of the 90 contour line in N.19 from which to bring fire to bear on NEUVILLE VITASSE TRENCH and assist the advance of 30th Division.

B Pakenham
Lieut-Colonel,
General Staff.

Head Qrs. 56th Divn.
29th March, 1917.

Copies to -
167th Inf. Bde.
168th Inf. Bde.
169th Inf. Bde.
VII Corps.
 "   " Arty.
 "   " H.A.
C.R.A.
C.R.E.
1/5th Cheshire Regt.
A.D.M.S.
"Q"
A.P.M.

193rd Div. M.G.Coy.
56th Div. Signals.
56th Div. Train.
Div. M.G.Officer.
Div. Gas Officer.
D.A.D.O.S.
4th Aust. Div. Supply Column.
No. 2 Ammn. Sub Park.
G.O.C.
A.D.C.
War Diary.
File.

SECRET.

56th Divn. No.G.A.58.

C.R.A.
C.R.E.
167th Infantry Brigade.
168th Infantry Brigade.
169th Infantry Brigade.
1/5th Cheshire Regiment.
A.D.M.S.
56th Div. "Q"
----

1. The attached paper shows work required in the immediate future on the new Divisional front.

2. Preparation for the offensive must be pressed on with all speed, as very short notice may be given for operations to commence.

3. R.A. work has not been included. The C.R.A. will draw up a programme and forward a copy to Div. H.Qrs.

4. Weekly Progress Reports will be furnished by the Infantry Brigade holding the Line, the C.R.A., C.R.E. and A.D.M.S. to show how the work affecting them has progressed.

The reports to be submitted weekly to Divn. Head Qrs. on Wednesday by 6 p.m.

5. The Infantry Brigade holding the line will be responsible for work on C.Ts. in the captured German Line, the upkeep of fighting trenches, and the construction of assembly trenches or the opening up of such old trenches as may be necessary, etc.

The C.R.A. will be responsible for all work on Gun Positions, O.Ps. and T.M. Emplacements (if T.M's are used), ammunition, stores and accommodation for R.A. personnel.

All other work including dugouts, road repair and construction, laying of tramways, etc. will be arranged for by Div. H.Q. with the C.R.E.

The R.E. will supply the necessary supervision required by the G.O.C. Brigade in the Line, who will demand R.E. stores through their attached Field Coy.

Head Qrs. 56th Divn.
24th March, 1917.

B Pakenham
Lieut-Colonel,
General Staff.

Details.	Nature of Work.	Remarks.
(A). C.Ts. **RIGHT BRIGADE.** 1. STOCKHAUSEN WEG. 2. DREISBACH WEG. 3. STRASON WEG. 4. GRUNDHERR LANE.	To be reclaimed.	PRIORITY to be given to existing trenches.
LEFT BRIGADE. 1. FALLOW LANE, EASTERN SIDE of CIRCULAR REDOUBT (M.11.d. and M.17.b.) to BATTERY Position in M.17.b. - thence to MANCHE Tr. at M.18.c.5.8.	FALLOW LANE to be reclaimed. PREUSSEN WEG to be reclaimed all through.	
2. FALLOW LANE, EASTERN SIDE of CIRCULAR REDOUBT, BATTERY POSITION in M.17.b. - thence across PREUSSEN WEG at M.18.c.5.5. thence BATTERY TR. to M.12.d.8.0. - thence WILLY TRENCH at M.18.b.2.8.	Remainder of work enumerated in Column 1 to be dug.	
3. MANOIR TR. at M.18.d.2.6. - M.18.d.3.6. and 5.0.from M.18.d. 3.5. to DEODAR TR. M.18.d.5.2.		
4. Join ONE TR. at M.18.b.5.3. with DEODAR TR. at M.18.b.7.2.		
(B) TRAMWAY. Suggested route M.10.b.5.2. M.10.d.5.0. thence along P.9 C.T.; to SUNKEN ROAD M.16.b.9.6. - thence along SUNKEN ROAD.	Lifting track from AGNY - HAVANNAH T.M.Rly. relaying same. Digging out P.9 C.T. and revetting it to SUNKEN ROAD.	C.R.E. to reconnoitre for best site. Labour available from Pioneer Battalion & R.E. Last in order of Priority, only to be undertaken when all other preparations are complete.

Details.	Nature of Work.	Remarks, and troops responsible for work.
(C) Dugout accommodation round ACHICOURT.	Completion of Elephant Shelters on ACHICOURT – AGNY RAILWAY.	To be completed as soon as possible – Pioneer Battalion.
(D) Advanced Dressing Station ACHICOURT.	Completion of Scheme.	R.A.M.C. under C.R.E.
(E) Roads. Leading forward.	Clearing for Light Traffic.	Pioneer Battalion under C.R.E.. Infantry parties as available.
(F) Dumps, Brigade and Battalion.	For stores rations and water.	As required by assaulting Brigades. Brigade in the Line.
(G) Cables.	Adapting British and German system to give buried communication between Div. H.Q., Brigade H. Qrs., C.R.A. and A.A.Groups and Div.O.P. at M.16.b.40.75	O.C., Signals assisted by Infantry Working Parties.
(H) Divisional O.P.M.16.b.40.75.	Complete existing dugouts.	Div. Observers. Under R.E.supervision.
(I) Clearing our wire.	Making lanes in our wire for assaulting troops.	This applies to all wire behind our front line. Lines of wire not under direct observation may be cleared at once. The thinning of wire in the Front Line system is to be undertaken gradually.
(J) Assembly trenches.	Left Brigade (1). M.18.d.2.9. to MANOIR TR. M.18.d.15.60. (2). M.18.d.10.40 to M.18.d.00.20. (3). M.18.d.35.60 to M.18.d.2.1. (4). M.18.d.6.3. to M.24.b.45.90. (5). M.18.d.80.70 to M.24.b.55.85.	The particulars of assembly trenches required by 167th Brigade are not to hand, but will be issued later.
(K) Ladders.	1000) To commence with.	C.R.E. assaulting Brigades will make known their exact requirements.
(L) Bridges.	250.)	

NOTES. 512th Field Coy. R.E. are making a census of all dugouts in BEAURAINS.
513th Field Coy. R.E. are making a census of all dugouts in Trench System.

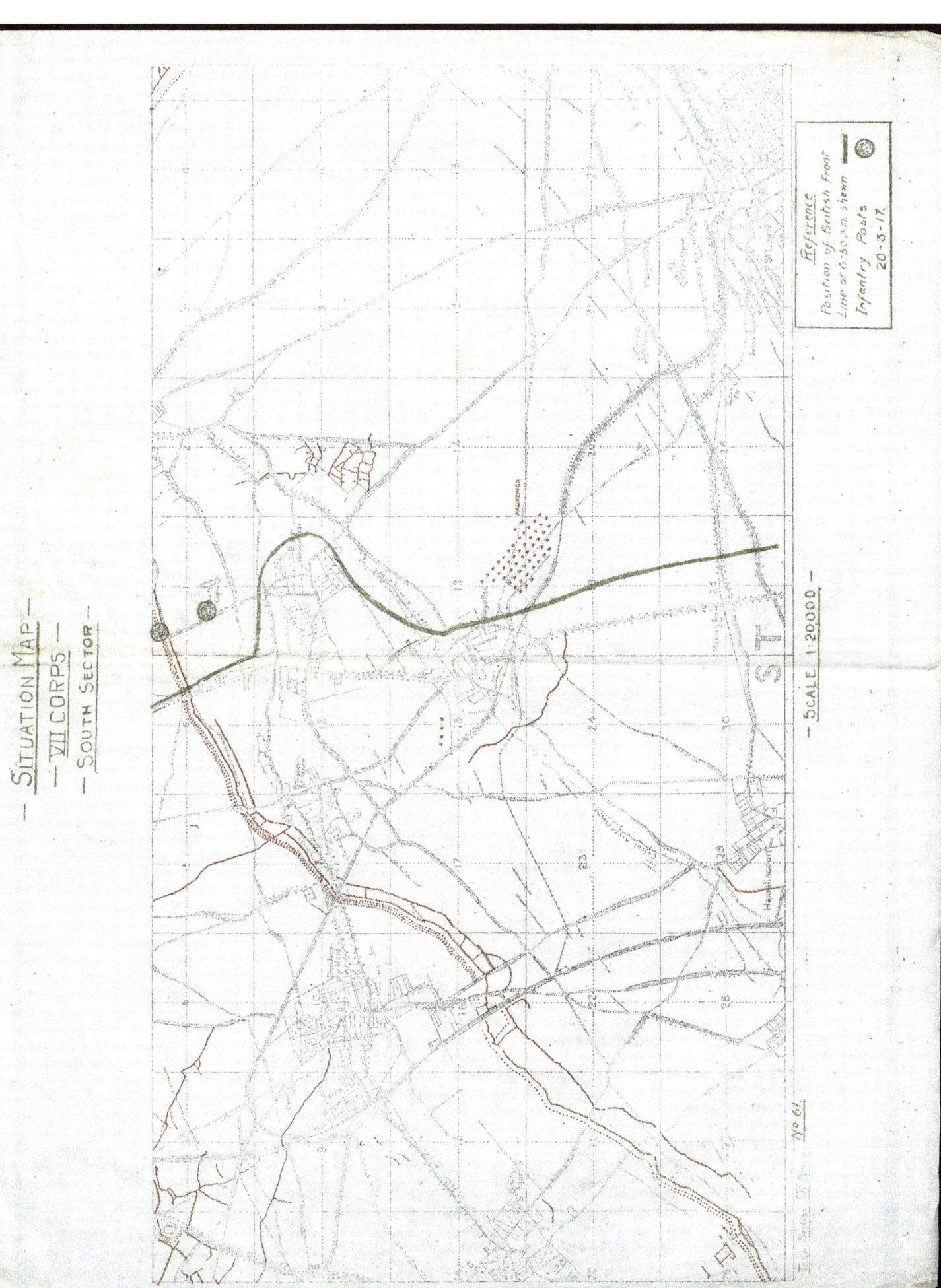

SECRET.   Copy No. 19.

56th DIVISION WARNING ORDER No. 77.

22nd March, 1917.

Reference attached Maps 1/20,000 No. 7444/2 (A)
& 1/5,000 NEUVILLE VITASSE   (B).

Objective of 56th Division. 1. With reference to 56th Division No. G.A.43 of 19th inst. -the task of the 56th Division will be :-

(a). 1st Objective - the capture of the Blue Line shewn on attached Map "A".

(b). 2nd Objective - the capture of the portion of the COJEUL SWITCH Line situated within the Divisional boundaries, and the establishment of a line approximately as shown by the Brown Line on the attached Map "A".

Method of Attack. 2. The attack will be carried out by 167th Infantry Brigade on the right and by 168th Infantry Brigade on the left.

Objectives & Dividing Line between Assaulting Brigades. 3. The objectives of 167th and 168th Infantry Brigades and the dividing line between them are shown on the attached Map "A".
The dividing line in NEUVILLE VITASSE Village is shown in detail on Map "B".

Programme of Attack of VII Corps. 4. The probable programme of attack is as follows :-

At Zero - VI Corps to assault, so as to bring it level with left of VII Corps.

At Zero + 2 hours - 14th and 56th Divisions to assault and capture the Blue Line.

There will be a pause of 4 hours on this line, during which the 30th Division is to move up to the Blue Line.

At Zero + 6 hours 40 minutes - 30th, 56th & 14th Divisions to assault and advance to the Brown Line.

N.B.- The above programme is liable to modification.

Assembly Areas. 5. The Assembly Areas for 167th & 168th Infantry Brigades respectively lie between the boundaries shown on the attached Map "A" and the old German front line.

The Assembly Area for the 169th Infantry Brigade (in Divisional Reserve) is bounded on the N & S by the Divisional Boundaries, by the old British front line on the East and by the ARRAS - AGNY Railway (inclusive) on the West.

/6.

2.

Tanks.	6.	Four tanks will probably be allotted to the Division. Detailed orders for their employment will be issued later.
Gas.	7.	"A" Company Special Brigade R.E. will probably be available for projecting drums at least 24 hours prior to the assault. Detailed orders for this Company will be issued later.
Action of Divnl. Reserve.	8.	The Divisional Reserve (169th Infantry Brigade) will be held in readiness to move forward from Zero + 2 hours.
Artillery.	9.	The following Artillery will be under the Command of C.R.A., 56th Division :-

```
           56th Div. Arty.              36 guns    12 Howitzers.
           21st    "    "               36   "     12      "
           293rd Army F.A.Bde.          18   "      2      "
           1 Bty. 232nd F.A.Bde.         6   "

                              Total     96 guns &  26 Howitzers.
```

The detailed Artillery plan and barrage map will be issued later.

Headquarters of Brigades. 10. Infantry Brigade H.Qrs. will be as follows :-

   167th Infantry Brigade in German dugout -
                             approximately M.10.b.6.
   168th Infantry Brigade in German dugout -
                             approximately M.10.d.9.9.
   169th Infantry Brigade in dugout in British lines -
                                            M.3.b.35.95.

Divisional H.Q. 11. Divisional H.Q. will remain at BEAUMETZ.

12. ACKNOWLEDGE.

B. Pakenham
Lieut-Colonel,
General Staff.

Head Qrs. 56th Divn.

Issued at 11.30 p.m.

```
Copy No. 1.  167th Infantry Bde.     14. Div. M.G. Officer.
         2.  168th Infantry Bde.     15. "A" Coy. Spec.Bde.R.E.
         3.  169th Infantry Bde.     16. Heavy Section M.G.
         4.  C.R.A.                                    Corps.
         5.  C.R.E.                  17. G.O.C.
         6.  "Q"                     18. 193rd M.G.Coy.
         7.  A.D.M.S.                19. War Diary.
         8.  A.P.M.                  20. File.
      9 & 10. VII Corps.             21. O.C., Signals.
        11.  14th Division.
        12.  30th Division.
        13.  Div. Gas Officer.
```

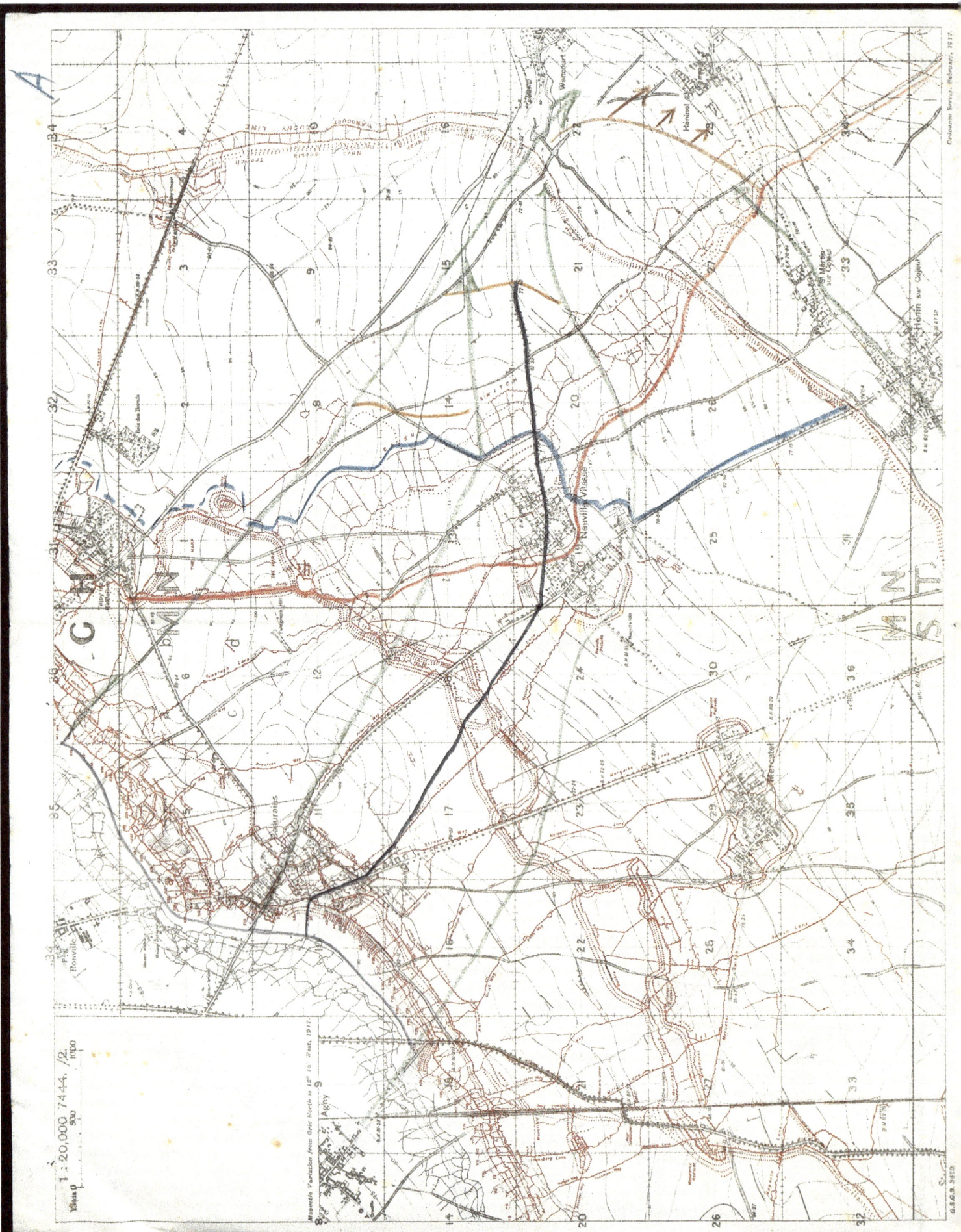

SECRET.   *War Diary*   Copy No. 20

56th DIVISION ORDER No. 78.

28th March 1917

Ref. SHEET 51 C. and Attached Sketch Map.

1. On the night of the 31st/1st, 167th and 168th Machine Gun Companies will relieve the 169th Machine Gun Company in the Line.
    On relief 169th M.G.Coy. will remain in ACHICOURT and retain their present billets.
    The Headquarters of the 167th M.G.Coy. will be at AGNY, and those of the 168th M.G.Coy. at ACHICOURT.

2. On April 1st and night of April 1st/2nd, the 167th and 168th Infantry Brigades will relieve the 169th Infantry Brigade in the Line.

3. Brigade frontages are shown on the attached Sketch Map.

4. The dispositions of 167th and 168th Brigades after the relief of 169th Brigade will be as follows :—

    167th Brigade Headquarters   M.3.d.2.2.
        "A" Battalion   in the Line.
        "B" Battalion   in Support.
        "C" Battalion   )
                &   )   AGNY.
        7th Middlesex Regt)

    168th Brigade Headquarters   M.3.b.35.95.
        "A" Battalion   in the Line.
        "B" Battalion   in Support.
        "C" & "D" Battalions in Reserve in ACHICOURT.

5. Brigades will move as per attached March Table.

6. Details of relief will be arranged by Brigadier-Generals Commanding concerned.

7. The 169th Brigade will, on relief, move :—

    Brigade Headquarters, 169th T.M.Battery and
        3 Battalions to MONCHIET.
        1 Battalion to BEAUMETZ-les-LOGES.

    Route - WAILLY - R.8.c.8.2. - Main ARRAS-DOULLENS
            Road - BEAUMETZ.

8. Q.M. Stores and 1st Line Transport of 167th Infantry Brigade will be accommodated at AGNY.CH.

9. Q.M. Stores and 1st line transport of 168th Brigade will be accommodated at ACHICOURT.

10. ACKNOWLEDGE.

Head Qrs. 56th Divn.   W.Brook Captain
28th March, 1917.   Lieut-Colonel,
                Issued at 10 p.m.   General Staff.

Copy No.					
1.	167th Inf.Bde.	8.	"Q"	18.	G.O.C.
2.	168th Inf.Bde.	9.	A.P.M.	*19.	A.D.C.
3.	169th Inf.Bde.	10.	193rd Div.M.G.Coy.	20.	War Diary.
4.	C.R.A.	11.	56th Div.Signals.	21.	File.
5.	C.R.E.	*12.	56th Div. Train.	22.	VII Corps.
6.	1/5th Chos.Regt.	13.	Div. M.G.Officer.		
7.	A.D.M.S.	*14.	Div. Gas Officer.		
		*15.	D.A.D.O.S.		
		*16.	4th Aust.Div.Supply Col.		
		*17.	No.2 Ammn.Sub Park.		

* Sketch map not attached.

MARCH TABLE issued with 56th DIVISION ORDER No. 78.

Unit.	From.	To.	Remarks.
March 31st. 167th & 169th Machine Gun Coys.	Present area.	Line.	Route. BEAUMETZ - Main ARRAS - DOULLENS Road to R.8.c.8.2. - thence WAILLY - AGNY. 167th Machine Gun Coy. to clear BEAUMETZ by 10 a.m. 168th Machine Gun Coy. not to enter BEAUMETZ before 10.30 a.m.
April 1st 167th Bde. (less 1 Bn.)	MONCHIET	Line.	via BEAUMETZ - RIVIERE - WAILLY. 167th Infantry Brigade will clear BEAUMETZ by 3 p.m.
168th Bde. (less 2 Bns.)	GOUY-en-ARTOIS	Line.	168th Infantry Brigade will not enter BEAUMETZ before 3.15 p.m. No troops, other than Lewis Gun Teams, will cross the old British front line before 7 p.m.

"War Diary"

SECRET 56th Divn. G.3/82.

AMENDMENT to 56th DIVISION ORDER No.78.

In March Table issued with 56th Div. Order No. 78, routes shown in column of remarks are cancelled.

All troops will now move via BEAUMETZ - Main ARRAS - DOULLENS Road - road junction L.29.d.- ACHICOURT.

A.P.M., 56th Division will provide special passes for all 1st line transport.

ACKNOWLEDGE.

B. Pakenham
Lieut-Colonel,
General Staff.

Head Qrs. 56th Divn.
29th March, 1917.

Copies to 167th Inf. Bde.
        168th Inf. Bde.
        169th Inf. Bde.
        C.R.A.
        C.R.E.
        1/5th Ches. Regt.
        A.D.M.S.
        "Q"
        A.P.M.
        193rd Div. M.G.Coy.
        56th Div. Signals.
        56th Div. Train.
        Div. M.G.Officer.
        Div Gas Officer.
        D.A.D.O.S.
        4th Aust. Div.Supply Column.
        No. 2 Ammn. Sub Park.
          G.O.C.
          A.D.C.
          War Diary
          VII Corps
          File.

Location Table.

March		13	14	15	16	17	18	19	20	21	22	23	24	25
Div. H.Q		LE CAUROY						BEAUMETZ						
	H.Q.	SUS-ST-LEGER												
	1. Ldn.	WARLUZEL										MONCHIET		
167 Bde	3 Ldn.	SUS-ST-LEGER										MONCHIET		
	7 Mx	HUMBERCOURT		DAINVILLE								MONCHIET		
	8 Mx	SUS-ST-LEGER										AGNY		
	H.Q.	IVERGNY										MONCHIET		
	4 Ldn.	BEAUDRICOURT										GOUY-en-ARTOIS		
168 Bde	12 "	IVERGNY										BEAUMETZ-les-LOGES		
	13 "	IVERGNY										GOUY-en-ARTOIS		
	14 "	IVERGNY										GOUY-en-ARTOIS		
	H.Q.	GOUY-en-ARTOIS DAINVILLE					Adv. ACHICOURT G 36c.16.	ACHICOURT Q 36c.16.		ACHICOURT M.11 M 3b 3.9.				
	2 Ldn.	ACHICOURT	Line							R.	ACHICOURT SUPPORT		SUPPORT	
169 Bde	5 "	FOSSEUX	DAINVILLE ARRAS (Rue Frederic de Georges)				R	R	R	R	R	L		
	9 "	GOUY-en-ARTOIS ARRAS (Rue Aden)					ACHICOURT		L	L	L	L	L	R	
	16 "	SIMENCOURT	ACHICOURT					BEAUMETZ					R	ACHICOURT
Div. Arty.	250 Bde	LUCHEUX	GOUY-en-ARTOIS											
	281 "	SIMENCOURT	SIMENCOURT	Line										
Pioneers.		ARRAS K.15.c.4.2.	Line					ARRAS (Rue des Trois Filloires)		ARRAS Boulevard Cnapsal				

Line in Red.   SUPPORT } BLACK.   BACK AREAS, GREEN.
                RESERVE

Appendix B

Location Table.

March	1	2	3	4	5	6	7	8	9	10	11	12
Div. H.Q.	LA GORGUE	—	—	—	—	WILLEMAN	—	LE CAUROY	—	—	—	—
167 Bde. H.Q.	LAVENTIE (COCKSHY HOUSE)				LESTREM		PERNES	FRANEFCOURT	SUS-St-LEGER			WARLUZEL
1 Ldn.	Pont du Hem.						SACHIN	HERICOURT	IVERGNY			
3 Ldn.	R	R	R	R								
7 Mx.	RIEZ BAILLEUL				St VENANT		TANGRY	CROIX	SUS-St LEGER			ITUMBERCOURT
8 Mx.	L	L	L	L			BOYAVAL	CROISETTE	BEAUVOIRCOURT			
							FLORINGHEM	GAUCHIN	SUS-St LEGER		Marching Parties	
168 Bde. H.Q.	Les HUIT MAISONS				CENSE DE RAUX				MERVILLE	Train to IVERGNY		
4 Ldn.	FOSSE				L	L	L	L	BOUT DEVILLE	LE SOUICH	10th St VENANT BEAUVOIRCOURT	
12 Ldn.	R	R	R	R								
13 Ldn.	L	L	L	L	SENESCHAL FARM		LESTREM		LESTREM	LE SOUICH	11th VAL HUON IVERGNY	
											12th LE CAUROY area.	
14 Ldn.	CROIX BARBEE				CROIX BARBEE				FOSSE	IVERGNY		IVERGNY
					R	R	R	R	VIEILLE CHAPELLE	BREVILLERS		
169 Bde. H.Q.	LESTREM	St FLORIS	PERNES	OEUF	LE QUESNOY	BONNIERES	SUS-St LEGER	GOUY-en-ARTOIS				
2 Ldn.	LESTREM	St VENANT	FIEFS	MOULETTE	CHERIENNE	FORTEL	IVERGNY	MONCHIET				
5 Ldn.	VIEILLE CHAPELLE	"	TANGRY	FILLIEVRES	LE BOYOLE	BOIRE-au-BOIS	IVERGNY	FOSSEUX				
9 Ldn.	LA GORGUE	"	SACHIN	WILLEMAN	REGNAVILLE	ROUGEFAY	IVERGNY	GOUY-en-ARTOIS				
16 Ldn.	BOUT DEVILLE	"	FLORINGHEM	OEUF	LE QUESNOY	BONNIERES	SUS-St LEGER	SIMENCOURT				
Div. Arty. H.Q.	LA GORGUE					St VENANT	St ANDRÉ	ANVIN	FILLIEVRES		LUCHEUX	
280 Bde.	In the line					LIGNY-lez-AIRE			BOUBERS		LUCHEUX	
281 Bde.	"										SIMENCOURT	
Pioneers	LAVENTIE				Bus to ARRAS Kisc 4.2.	MERVILLE						

Line in Red. RESERVE } BLACK BACK AREAS, GREEN
SUPPORT

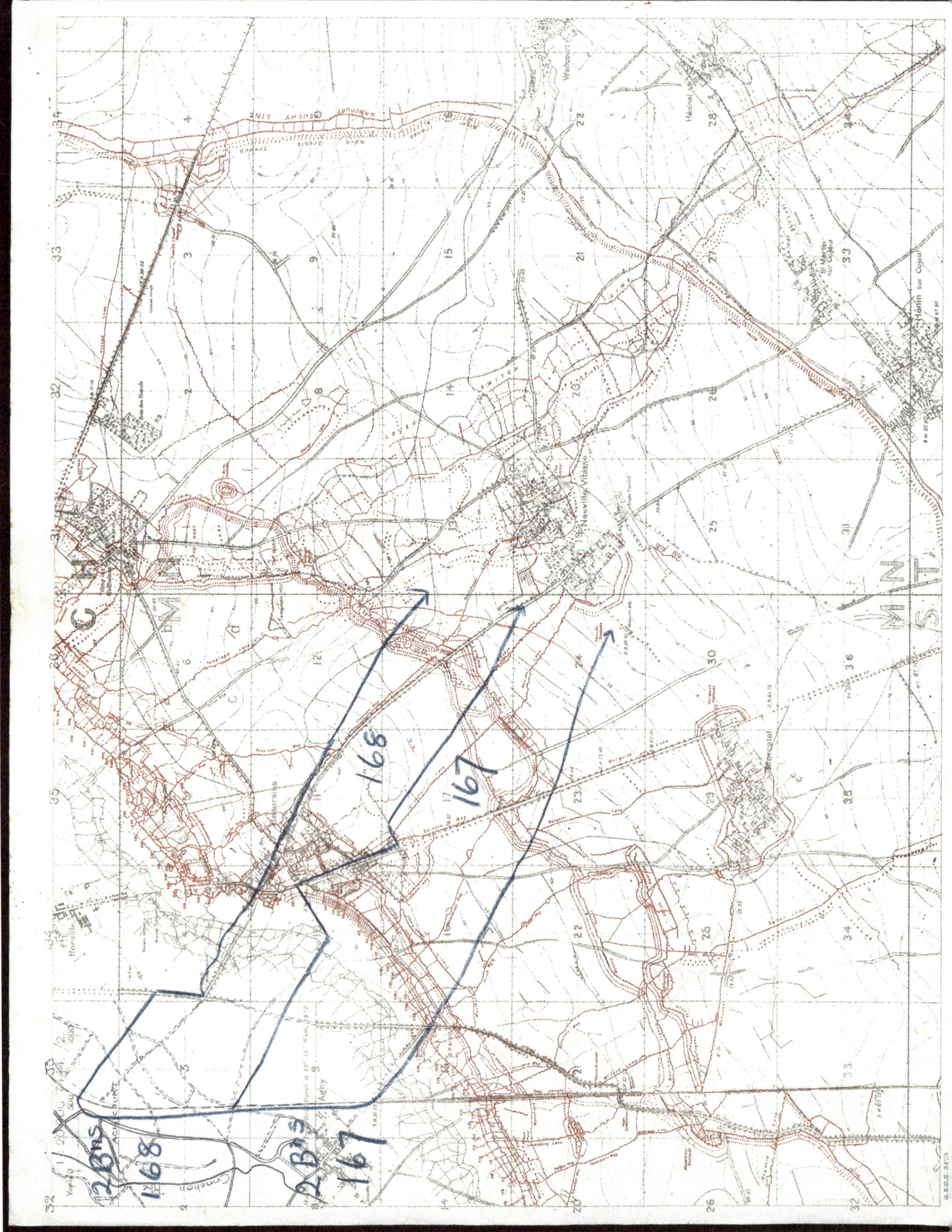

LOCATION TABLE.

March		26	27	28	29	30	31	April 1	2	3	4	5
Div. H.Q.		Beaumetz les Loges										
167 Inf. Bde.	H.Q.	Monchiet										
	1st Lon. Regt.	Monchiet										
	3rd "	Monchiet										
	7th Mx "	Agny										
	8 "	Monchiet										
168 Inf. Bde.	H.Q.	Gouy-en-Artois										
	4th Lon. Regt.	Beaumetz les Loges	O.B.L.									
	12th "	Gouy										
	13th "	Gouy										
	14th "	Gouy	Agny									
169 Inf. Bde.	H.Q.	Achicourt 27 & 28		R	R	R	R					
	2nd Lon. Regt.	L		L	L							
	5th " "	L										
	9th " "	Achicourt				Achicourt						
	16th " "	Support				Support						
Div Arty	H.Q.	Beaumetz les Loges										
	280 Bde	Line										
	281 "	Line										
Pioneers		Arras Boulevard Crespel										

Appendix C

56th DIVISIONAL TACTICAL PROGRESS REPORT No. 126.

from 8.0 a.m. 28th February to 8.0 a.m. 1st March, 1917.

On receipt of current copy of Divisional Tactical Progress Report in the trenches, previous copy to be destroyed.

PART I OPERATIONS.

RIGHT SECTION. - Our Artillery has been active during the last 24 hours, carrying out several schemes of retaliation for enemy T.M. fire. Stokes Mortars caused much damage to the enemy trenches and wire. H.T.M's secured direct hits on M.G.E's and T.M'Es. M.G's carried out organised shoot between 6 and 11 p.m., firing 12000 rounds on to LA TOURELLE Cross Roads and DISTILLERY. Detailed reports of enemy wire brought in by Patrols. Our Snipers claimed two hits.

CENTRE SECTION. - Group Artillery fired in co-operation with the Heavies, dispersed enemy parties in the open, and silenced hostile T.M.'s. M.T.M's and L.T.M's fired with effect on new enemy work. Patrols report that there is evidence of much recent work on the enemy wire and that all the gaps made by our T.M's have been filled in.

LEFT SECTION. - Our guns co-operated with the Heavies and fired on working parties. A very successful shoot was carried out by the M.T.M's. 12000 rounds fired by our M.G's on to enemy communications during the night. An enemy sniper was hit and lay over the parapet till his body was pulled in.

PART II INTELLIGENCE

RIGHT SECTION. - Enemy artillery was fairly quiet, but there was a good deal of T.M. fire along the front. Some damage was done to HUN Street and front line parapet was breached near SHETLAND C.T. Enemy M.G's were unusually active during the night. There is a dump of corrugated iron and timber at S.11.a.3.3.

CENTRE SECTION. - Hostile artillery was quiet, but T.M.'s fired frequently during the day, and our wire has been slightly damaged in places on the left Battalion front. Movement was normal, except between 4-30 and 5-0 p.m. when about 30 men in ones and twos and some horses passed TRAMWAY Corner. There was considerable movement around ROAD JUNCTION N.27.a.6.2. A 6 horsed wagon and other transport was seen on road in T.3.a. about 4 p.m.

LEFT SECTION. - Hostile artillery were quieter than usual and restricted to 77 m-m shells. Hostile M.G's were active at intervals during the day and night. No transport could be heard last night, which is unusual.

SMOKE. - S.5.b.58.20 - S.11.a.93.32 Dug-out - S.22.a.9.1 behind ruin - the SUGAR Factory at MARQUILLIES.- HERLIES CHIMNEY N.31.a.32.22 Dug-out - N.21.a.6.6 - N.20.b.30.55 suspected H.Q. - N.27.c.25.95 HOUSE.

H.Q. 56th Division.
1st March, 1917.

John D. Crosthwaite
Captain,
Intelligence, General Staff.

56th DIVISIONAL TACTICAL PROGRESS REPORT No. 127
from 8.0 a.m. 1st March to 8.0 a.m 2nd March 1917.

All Summaries of Intelligence and Orders are of value to the
enemy, if captured, and are not to be taken into action.
On receipt of current Divisional Tactical Progress Report in
the trenches, previous copy to be burnt.

PART I OPERATIONS.

FME. DU BOIS SECTION.- Our artillery dispersed several enemy working parties seen during the day, viz :- A party of 12 men working on trench running N.W. through S.24.c. and d. - Party of 4 men repairing telephone wires at T.2.c.55.88., and a party of 20 men in clean fatigue carrying timber in S.29.a. Registration on various points in the enemy lines was effected, and several hostile T.Ms. reported active were silenced.

Our T.Ms. bombarded the enemy trenches at S.22.a.68.70. where an enemy post is suspected. Other points fired on were S.16.c.93.35., S.16.a.72.80. head of MITZI C.T. and support lines in S.10.c. and d. The shooting was uniformly good and much damage was done.

Our M.Gs. displayed their usual activity during the night.

Our snipers fired at Germans at the following points :-
S.11.a.40.20., believed hit - S.16.c.90.40. man disappeared - S.16.a.85.80. man disappeared, S.22.a.78.10 hit in the arm, S.16.c. 80.45. killed.

NEUVE CHAPELLE SECTION.- Our artillery carried our a group programme in co-operation with the Heavies on MIN DU PIETRE - M.30.c.85.90 - M.30.c.70.75., T.1.b., N.32.a. and S.6.a.15.98. Shooting was very good. Hostile working parties were dispersed at N.32.c. 10.75., T.2.c.55.90, and T.1.b.60.20.

Our T.Ms. destroyed a M.G.E. at M.30.c.55.70.; also new enemy work at M.36.a.30.25. The hostile sentry post at M.36.a.40.65. received a sharp burst from our Stokes Mortars. A periscope which had been seen there was hurriedly removed.

FAUQUISSART SECTION.- Reports not yet received

PART II INTELLIGENCE.

Visibility excellent throughout the day.

FME.DU BOIS SECTION.-

One of our patrols visited the supposed sap at S.10.c. 95.30. and reported it to be merely a drain. Patrols out on our Right Front reported the enemy to be very much on the alert, and they were repeatedly fired at by hostile M.Gs. They located 2 M.Gs. mounted on the enemy parapet at S.22.c.55.35 and 80.20. and another M.G. Gun at S.16.c.90.70.

Hostile artillery were fairly active. The area near OXFORD STREET, CHURCH REDOUBT and "B" Line S.5.a. was shelled about mid-day. A Howitzer was seen to fire from the ORCHARD around the FME DU BIEZ - S.12.c.2.2. The shell which seemed to be of large calibre passed overhead towards CROIX BARBEE. Enemy 5.9" Hows. shelled one of our batteries near M.19 and 20 continuously during the day.

Hostile T.Ms. were much quieter, but his M.Gs. were very active. One was located at S.11.a.08.12.

New work has been done on the enemy trench at S.16.d. 20.65. and S.10.c.98.15.

A new stretch of wire 300 yards long has been put out in front of the enemy trenches opposite LES BRULOT S.5.d. During the night the enemy placed a number of coils of wire at S.10.d.50.30.

There appears to be a trench not marked on the map running along the N.W. side of the LORGIES RD. in S.24.c and d. Much work was seen in progress on this trench during the day. At 12.30 p.m. three parties of 20 men each were seen apparently being exercised in squad drill in a field at about S.25.d. central.

Considerable movement was seen on the light railway in T.2.a. and d. a light engine being seen and several parties of men. Small parties of men were seen on the LA BASSEE RD. at S.17.d.55.05. There is a large mound of earth probably a dugout at T.2.d.65.75. On this mount is a blue flag with a white centre. Enemy were seen pumping at S.10.d.70.40. A man was seen in the tree at S.5.d.75.00.

/Three

Three men wearing white brassards were seen in the ruins at S.23.b.4.4. Considerable amount of transport was seen on the road at T.8.b. and several trains were seen at ILLIES.

Smoke was seen S.5.d.40.30 and 65.40
S.13.c.98.03
S.17.a.20.52.
S.12.d.80.75.
S.18.c.49.85.
S.23.d.40.25.
& T.8.b.15.60.

NEUVE CHAPELLE SECTION.- Our patrols visited the taped trench at M.30.a. 70.85. - no signs of work could be found. The Craters were also examined.

A patrol visited the enemy trench at M.30.a.40.15 and reported hearing an enemy trench patrol. Other patrols did not come into contact with the enemy. The enemy frequently bombed his wire during the night.

Hostile artillery were very active, firing on to TILLELOY C.T. and also counter-battery work. A gas shell is reported to have fallen near GRANTS POST - M.23.d. A smell of phosgene was detected.

Hostile T.Ms. were fairly active during the day, and hostile M.Gs. swept our parapet frequently during the night.

Much new work has been done on the AUBERS DEFENCES about N.21.d.1.0. A working party seen there yesterday was dispersed.

Between 4 and 5.30 p.m. continuous movement was observed at TRAMWAY CORNER N.26.c. Some tape can be seen on the parapet at CLARA'SFAN at N.19.b.08.38. Two new direction boards are visible at N.32.c.0.1. where there appears to be a strong point or Redoubt. Usual movement was seen in N.32.c. and in the ruined house at M.30.d.85.85.

Smoke was seen at M.30.b.20.50. dugout, and house at N.32.c. 0.2.

Three hostile observation balloons were up during the afternoon and appeared to be directing the fire of their heavy guns, flashes of signalling apparatus being seen from one of the cars. Bearings were taken on these balloons as follows :-

From C.R.A's House (M.18.c.85.40) bearings 130°, 142° 40'- 146° 30'
" GRANTS POST (M.23.d.3.2.) " 123°, 142°.
" BRISTOL O.P. " 143°, & 158°
" SNOWDON O.P. (N.13.a.8.8.) " 137° 30', 152° & 158° 30'.

All these are true bearings. These shew balloons to have been at U.13.a. (SAINGHIN) and T.23.a. (MARQUILLIES).

FAUQUISSART SECTION.- More earth has been thrown up on to the parapet of MOSSY C.T. at N.20.b.30.55. The usual movement was seen on the tracks in N.15.c., N.21.a. and around the Dump in N.21.b. Individual men were seen on the track at N.14.d.85.65.

Smoke was seen at N.15.c.05.70. trench.
N.14.d.97.63. IRMA C.T.
N.27.c.20.95. House.
N.20.b.12.40. dugout.

(Reported by Div.Observers.)

Head Qrs. 56th Divn.
2nd March, 1917.

H.C.Hrald
Lieutenant,
Intelligence, General Staff.

56th DIVISIONAL TACTICAL PROGRESS REPORT No. 128.
from 8.0 a.m 2nd March to 8.0 a.m 3rd March, 1917.

All Summaries of Intelligence and Orders are of value to the enemy,
if captured, and are not to be taken into action.
On receipt of current Divisional Tactical Progress Report in the
Trenches, previous copy to be burnt.

PART I OPERATIONS.

FAUQUISSART SECTION.- Our artillery fired on to movement seen at various portions of the enemy line.

Our T.Ms. bombarded the enemy front line in N.19.c. - much water being thrown up.

Our M.Gs. fired along the RUE D'ENFER during the night.

NEUVE CHAPELLE SECTION.- Our artillery fired intermittently on selected targets during the day, and in retaliation to hostile artillery.

Our Stokes Mortars bombarded the enemy trench at M.30.a.55.55. where the enemy had been reported working. The parapet was breached. No retaliation.

Our M.Gs. carried out their usual indirect fire during the night.

At 8 a.m. our snipers fired at a German seen in the Crater at M.30.a.40.45. He commenced to run towards the enemy trenches. He was again fired on and believed to have been hit.

FME DU BOIS SECTION.- Our artillery were very active, and carried out several organised shoots.

Our Stokes Mortars bombarded the enemy trenches in S.22.a., S.16.c. and S.16.a. The suspected dugout at S.10.d.32.50. was destroyed.

Our Medium and Heavy T.Ms. fired on enemy trenches at S.10.d. and ruins at S.11.c. A direct hit was obtained on the hostile T.M. position at S.11.d.4.3. - shooting was good throughout. Our snipers hit one of two Germans seen looking over the parapet at S.11.a.20.20. They also fired at another German at S.16.a.60.70.

PART II INTELLIGENCE.   Visibility was fair.

FAUQUISSART SECTION.- One of our patrols, about 20 strong, entered the enemy trenches at N.19.a.3.5. It was found to be water logged and unused. They saw a hostile patrol filing through the trees at N.19.a. 3.2. Our party advanced and were challenged from the trench at N.19.a.30.35. The bad state of the ground prevented our patrol going further.

Hostile artillery fired a few shells on to our C.Ts. and our O.P. at C.R.A's House (M.18.d.0.4.).

An enemy L.T.M. fired from the direction of the Crater in M.13. d.9.7. upon RED LAMP CORNER.

Hostile M.Gs. were very active during the day and night with indirect fire, which is thought to be directed by an observer.

At 2.30 p.m. two Germans left the trench at N.19.d.2.6. carrying a coil of telephone wire, which they laid down, and disappeared at N.19.d.7.2.

Occasional movement was seen during the day on the RUE D'ENFER near the DISTILLERY - N.19.c. Usual movement was seen on the tracks in N.20.b.

NEUVE CHAPELLE SECTION.- One of our patrols was fired on from S.5.b.70.95. when near the enemy wire. Other patrols reported the Craters at M.30.a. to be unoccupied, and the enemy trench at M.30.c.55.10. to be occupied. Hostile artillery were fairly active yesterday, firing on to back areas during the afternoon. New wire is visible at several points near M.30.a.30.15. Work is continuing on the AUBERS DEFENCES at N.21.d.1.0. Considerable movement was seen in rear of the SHRINE at N.27.a.75.30. - a relief is suspected. A periscope was seen at M.36.a.30.25. and smoke at M.36.a.30.25. and M.36.b.75.55.

FME DU BOIS.- One of our patrols observed a hostile patrol which disappeared very quickly at S.22.c.35.10. The enemy was bailing water and firing Very lights at this point. Another sentry group was located at S.22.c.60.55., and a trench patrol was heard walking

/between

PART II INTELLIGENCE (Contd.)

FME. DU BOIS SECTION.-

walking between those points, and was challenged by these sentry groups. Another group is suspected at S.22.c.90.35.

Hostile artillery were active, distributing their fire on various points along the front. Twelve gas shells fell on the RUE DU BOIS, but only one exploded. A hostile 4.2" Battery was seen and bearings taken place it about S.18.c.9.4.

Hostile T.Ms. fired on the area near PORT ARTHUR, apparently in retaliation to our H.T.Ms.

A hostile M.G. is suspected at S.16.c.8.6.

New revetting can be seen at S.22.c.90.20. Six cupolas have been erected at S.22.b.80.10 and new wire at S.10.c.95.10.

A working party was seen digging at S.23.b.30.30. and six men at S.16.d.80.40. Several trains were seen during the day, and considerable movement on the roads, that on the road in T.8.a. was abnormal. There is a dump of trench boards and hurdles at S.22.b.40.90. also at S.22.d.60.90.

An O.P. or M.G.E. is visible in the house at S.24.c.40.05. The top of the German parapet North of FARME COUR D'AVOUE has wire along it. Several small parties were seen on the track from T.2.a.50.70. to T.1.b.60.05. A pathway apparently exists on the S.W. side of the LA BASSEE RD. in S.23.b.

Smoke was seen at S.23.d.40.25. house
      S.5.d.75.65.
      S.5.b.72.98.
        75.65.
      T.19.c.25.75.
      T.15.a.   chimney near FME. and USINE HOUSSIN.

      S.24.d.25.35.

Head Qrs. 56th Divn.
3rd March, 1917.

T.J.C.Heald
Lieutenant,
Intelligence, General Staff.

56th DIVISIONAL TACTICAL PROGRESS REPORT No. 129.
from 8. 0 a.m. 3rd March to 8. 0 a.m. 4th March, 1917.

All Summaries of Intelligence and Orders are of value to the enemy,
if captured, and are not to be taken into action.
On receipt of current Divisional Tactical Progress Report in the
trenches, previous copy to be burnt.

PART I OPERATIONS.
FME DU BOIS SECTION.- L.T.Ms. fired 200 rounds, damaging defences of FME. COUR D'AVOUE and also damging enemy front line at several points.   200 rifle grenades were fired on to MITZI O.T. and S.5.b. 6.2. during the night.   Snipers had several targets and claim hits.
NEUVE CHAPELLE SECTION.- L.T.Ms. cut wire during the night.
    M.Gs. fired 9000 rounds on enemy communications during the night.
FAUQUISSART SECTION.- Machine Guns carried out usual night firing.
    Working parties were dispersed by rifle fire.

PART II INTELLIGENCE.   Visibility very poor, and back areas only dimly visible at intervals during the day.
FME DU BOIS. SECTION. -   Enemy's wire was patrolled in S.22.c. and reported to be in very good condition.   Enemy working parties were heard at this point.   Rifle fire was opened from several points in enemy front line, and disused trench about S.16.c.8.5. on our patrol approaching this point.   A fighting patrol waited on the enemy parapet at S.22.c.65.90. with the intention of securing an identification from enemy working parties reported at this point, but no movement was observed.
    Enemy artillery was quiet during the day.   Their retaliation to our T.M. shoot being quickly silenced.
    Hostile M.Gs. were active during the night sweeping our front line and "B" line, and FORESTERS LANE.   M.Gs. were located at S.16.c.8.8. and S.22.c.8.0. and field guns fired on latter position.
    Enemy T.Ms. were quiet.
    A working party was seen   in the second line at S.16.b.60.85 - 40.05.   A breach in parapet at S.16.a.85.20. has been repaired. New sandbagging at S.22.c.78.42. S.16.b.6.5. - 6.7. and 0.6.
    Movement was normal during the day.   At noon a train was seen on the railway near ILLIES going South.
NEUVE CHAPELLE SECTION.- During the mist yesterday morning enemy line was visited at M.30.a.7.6. and found damaged almost passed repair. The line was also entered in rear of WINCHESTER CRATERS.
    During the night patrol moved to M.30.a.40.15. and patrolled 200 yds. South. without hearing any sign of the enemy.
FAUQUISSART SECTION.- Hostile M.T.Ms. fired 10 rounds on our trenches in N.13.c. and some rifle grenades on to RED LAMP SALIENT.
    Enemy M.Gs. were fairly active, firing intermittently during the day along RUE TILLELOY, and PICANTIN RD. - Approximate location - N.25.b.70.99.,   No unusual movement was noticed in the back areas.   Transport heard in the RUE D'ENFER about 5 a.m. as usual.   WICK SALIENT was entered during the night. The trench is only just recognisable and the wire forms no obstacle.   Another patrol reports VERY Lights being sent up from the enemy front line at N.14.b.20.85.

Head Qrs. 56th Divn.
4th March, 1917.

Captain,
Intelligence, General Staff.

56th DIVISIONAL TACTICAL PROGRESS REPORT No. 130.
from 8.0 a.m. 4th March to 8.0 a.m. 5th March, 1917.

All Summaries of Intelligence and Orders are of value to the enemy,
if captured, and are not to be taken into action.
On receipt of current copy of Divisional Tactical Progress Report
in the trench, previous copy to be destroyed.

PART I OPERATIONS.

FME DU BOIS. - L.T.Ms. fired 200 rounds during the day on suspected M.G.E. and snipers post in the front line. Our snipers were busy during the day, claiming several hits.

An enemy relief was suspected opposite this section and L.T.Ms. fired 500 rounds during the early part of the night on enemy front line and support line, with a large proportion of air bursts. 100 rifle grenades were fired on MITZI C.T. and 100 on S.5.b.6.2.

Our M.Gs. carried out a programme on enemy communications in the back areas.

NEUVE CHAPELLE. - L.T.Ms. caused considerable damage to enemy trenches at M.35.a.75.50. The usual night firing was carried out by M.Gs.

FAUQUISSART SECTION. - Our L.T.Ms. were active against BERTHA POST.

INTELLIGENCE - PART II.   Visibility very good.

FME DU BOIS SECTION. - An Officers' patrol examined enemy wire at QUINQUE RUE. It consists of heavily wired knife rests and is a good obstacle. Head of ADALBERT ALLEY appeared to be held by a strong post.

Hostile artillery - slightly active against "B" Line right sub-section - right Company H.Q., and CHURCH REDOUBT.

Ten rounds H.T.M. were fired near PORT ARTHUR.

Enemy M.Gs. were very active during the night, especially over OXFORD C.T. and EDGEWARE ROAD. A number of poles have been put up at 30 yd. intervals along the LA BASSEE/in S.23.b., possibly screening is intended here. Work on new trench at S.18.b.60.68 progresses very slowly. Parties about 30 strong each, were seen walking along the road at T.26.d.1.4. - eight parties were seen in all, and also two wagons. At 3 p.m. a number of small parties about 8 strong were seen on the FOURNES RD. Usual movement in T.2. A good deal of movement was seen over the whole area - parties of two and three, being seen on most tracks and roads at some time during the day

NEUVE CHAPELLE SECTION. - Hostile artillery was quiet during the day but fired a little during the early part of the night. A few T.M. Shells fell near MAUQUISSART CRATERS without doing any damage.

Working parties were dispersed by L.G. fire and artillery.

A good deal of work has been done recently on the HT POMMEREAU DEFENCES. New wire can be seen along enemy front line from M.35.d.9.4. to S.5.b.5.0.

A dead German was found by a patrol from the Right Bn. He had been dead some time - rifle, bayonet and sheath knife were brought in.

FAUQUISSART SECTION. - Enemy were very quiet throughout the day. An M.G. was again seen active from N.25.b.75.95. A sniper killed a German by MOSSY TRENCH.

A patrol moved up BEDFORD ST. towards enemy line. A party of enemy 10 strong who had been lying in front of their parapet disappeared into the trench. A buzzer sounded and in a minute three parties each about 10 strong got over their parapet and opened rapid fire on our patrol. A dyke full of water between the two patrols prevented our rushing the enemy and the patrol fell back without casualties. Enemy line was entered at N.14.a.5.0. C.T. and front line are full of water. Three stick bombs with caps removed were found on the parapet. Voices could be heard to the right and in front, and trucks were being pushed along the tramway to the right. Very Lights were sent up from enemy front line at N.14.a.9.6. At 3.30 p.m. a hostile 'plane attacked one of our F.E. scouts continuing the encounter to within 200 ft. of the ground, compelling our machine to land at X.4.c.9.4. A hostile 'plane went down our front line about LA BASSEE RD. at a height of about 300 ft. L.G. and rifle fire which was opened at once drive him off.

Head Qrs. 56th Divn.
5.2.17.

Captain,
Intelligence, General Staff

56th DIVISIONAL TACTICAL PROGRESS REPORT No. 1.
from 5 p.m. 20th March to 5 p.m. 21st March, 1917.

On receipt of current copy of Divisional Tactical Progress Report in the trenches, previous copy to be burnt.

PART I OPERATIONS.
BEAURAINS SECTION (169th Infantry Brigade)
Our line of advanced posts is now approximately, Light railway M.18.b.2.8. - M.18.b.5.4; DEODAR LANE M.18.d.7.8., VITASSE LANE and NEUVILLE LANE in M.24.b. to banks in M.24.c.
A patrol reached wire at M.18.d.10.25 and movement in trench was heard distinctly. PINE LANE is believed to be unoccupied.
A patrol discovered an enemy working party digging at M.18.d.7.8. We sent out a fighting patrol to attack it but party had gone when our men reached the place.
A patrol moved along outside the enemy's wire from M.24.b. 75.15. to M.24.d.95.33. The enemy was working all along this line and German orders were heard.
Our heavies were doing good shooting on the HARP and TELEGRAPH REDOUBT to-day. Shrapnel was fired over NEUVILLE VITASSE.
Machine guns are now in position. Two emplacements are completed and the third nearly finished.

PART II INTELLIGENCE.
BEAURAINS SECTION. (169th Infantry Brigade).
Hostile artillery has been engaged in registration on our new line. 20 or more 105 mm. H.E. fell on trench junction M.18.c.1.1. BEAURAINS was shelled more or less continuously during the night with light shells. Our old trenches were shelled during the morning and also the ACHICOURT - BEAURAINS Road near BEAURAINS.
Hostile M.Gs. opened fire on a party in the valley in M.24.a. from TELEGRAPH HILL. Men walking in the open behind our line were also fired at. Probable location: near first E. in NEUVILLE REDOUBT, house N.19.a.2.3.
Transport was seen going N.E. at 7.30 a.m. on road in N.34.a.
8 - 10 a.m. Individual men and small parties of not more than 4 men working all over the area. Nothing nearer our lines than NEUVILLE REDOUBT. Small parties seen on HENIN WANCOURT ROAD in N.21.d. and N.22.c. A party of about 20 men working at about Road Junction in N.24.d.
A man was seen working on a shelter at N.13.d.35.20. Men were previously seen carrying planks at this point.
10 - 12 noon. Work and movement seen at N.19.a.6.5., M.24.d. 80.55., N.13.c.85.55. Small parties of men carrying material seen in NEUVILLE VITASSE TRENCH, 3 men seen in trench N.19.b.70.15.
12 - 2 p.m. Party of 15 men seen on ridge T.5.d. Leading man seen carrying a small black flag about 3' - 2'. A large party of 150 men with one on horseback seen for a few minutes, they extended from the centre to cover 100 yards front and disappeared at about N.27.b.4.9.
2 - 4 p.m. 2 men seen in ruins at N.19.a.95.30. Four wagons seen going N.E. along road N.22.a. to N.21.d. Smoke was seen coming from behind ridge in direction of CROISELLES. Movement in NEUVILLE VITASSE has considerably lessened owing to our fire. At other places it continues.
Considerable movement was seen at various times on road from TELEGRAPH HILL and NEUVILLE VITASSE.
Smoke was seen coming from trench at N.24.b.9.3. Enemy A.A. guns reported yesterday at N.14.c.10.25 has been active. Observation balloons, three in all, were up to the N.E.
A light was seen in NEUVILLE VITASSE last night, apparently a hurricane lamp being carried about. We were unsuccessful in felling "aiming tree" in N.23.b. last night and it was registered again to-day. Buried cable marked on map was dug up near STRESOW WEG and tested. This will be put in a test box and labelled for future use.

Head Qrs. 56th Divn.   Intelligence,
22nd March, 1917.   General Staff.

SECRET.

56th DIVISIONAL TACTICAL PROGRESS REPORT No.2.
From 5 a.m. 22nd March to 5 a.m. 23 March, 1917.

On receipt of current copy of Divisional Tactical Progress Report, previous copy to be burnt.

PART I OPERATIONS.
BEAURAINS SECTION (169th Inf.Bde.)
(1) Since yesterday our outpost line has not changed, except that it was not found advisable to establish the post at M.18.b.25.90 owing to the field of fire being cut short by a 10 ft. bank. A post was made a#instead at M.18.b.20.55
(2). Patrols. (a) From the Q.V.R.
No patrols were sent out owing to the large number of men employed on covering parties during the establishment and improvement of Posts. Covering parties heard sounds of movement in NEUVILLE REDOUBT.
(b). From the Q.W.R.
An officers patrol investigated PINE TRENCH and found it held by the enemy from M.13.a.6.2. southwards.
(3). Artillery. More or less continuous and accurate fire was maintained by field guns and heavies on to TELEGRAPH HILL and NEUVILLE VITASSE. Much damage was done.

PART II INTELLIGENCE.
(1). Hostile Artillery. Fairly active. 77 mm. H.E. on to MERCATEL Road, NEUVILLE VITASSE Road and advanced Posts at M.24.a.3.0. BEAURAINS and roads in rear received an occasional shell. At 2 a.m. about 20 5.9's on to our front line in M.23.b.
(2). Hostile M.Gs. Were fairly active firing from direction of NEUVILLE VITASSE or TELEGRAPH HILL.
(3). Movement. During bombardment on our left a motor cyclist was seen on road through N.7.b. and N.7.d. also several groups of men. There was much less movement in NEUVILLE VITASSE. At 11.5 a.m. a wagon and two men were seen on road from TELEGRAPH HILL to NEUVILLE VITASSE, and other movement was seen here during the day.
Work was still continuing on the HENIN WANCOURT Line.
(4). Transport. Transport was heard behind the village at 6.15 am. and wagons were seen leaving NEUVILLE VITASSE going East at 6.45 am. One report states that a "caterpillar" was heard at this point.
(5). General. During bombardment on our left a large explosion took place in TILLOY, as if an ammunition dump was blown up. A small enemy patrol was seen about M.24.b.9.1. which made off as soon as it was challenged.
Three hostile balloons were observed behind ridge towards N.E. An enemy aeroplane flew very low along PREUSSEN WEG during the afternoon.
The H.T.M.Emplacement shown on Intelligence Maps at M.10.c. 8.4. has been left in good condition. There is a deep dugout with two entrances for the crew. The gun position, connected with the dugout by a flight of steps, has a large "funnel" or "hopper" opening. Although this shows plainly on all aerial photos it is quite undamaged by our guns.

[signature] Capt
Intelligence, General Staff.

Head Qrs. 56th Divn.
24th March, 1917.

SECRET.

56th DIVISIONAL TACTICAL PROGRESS REPORT NO.3.
from 5.0 a.m. 23rd March to 5.0 a.m. 24th March 1917.

On receipt of current copy of Divisional Tactical Progress Report in the trenches, previous copy to be burnt.

PART I OPERATIONS.
BEAURAINS SECTION (169th Inf.Bde.).
(1). Patrols. An Officers patrol from the Q.W.R. went down the light railway in M.18.a. to within 20 yards of PINE LANE. They saw sentries about every 20 yards one of whom struck a light. They found the trench wired. The wire is 3' high and not very deep.
(2). Artillery. Our guns fired with apparently good effect on to the trenches on TELEGRAPH HILL and in NEUVILLE VITASSE.
(3). Machine Guns. We fired a burst in reply to enemy M.G. on TELEGRAPH HILL.

PART II INTELLIGENCE.
BEAURAINS SECTION.(169th Inf.Bde.)
(1). Hostile Artillery. Registered new lines and strong points with 77, 105 and 5.9" shells. BEAURAINS was also shelled, one or two bursts of field gun fire were directed on to the hollow by the Sunken Road at M.16.b.8.8. The day was much quieter on the whole.
(2). M.G's. Fired on to MERCATEL and NEUVILLE VITASSE Roads during the night. A gun was seen firing from house at N.19.b.5.7.
(3). Transport. Motor and horse transport heard behind NEUVILLE VITASSE in the early morning.
A motor lorry was seen going East near the cross roads on the ridge in N.27.c.
(4). Movement. Small working parties and individual men were seen in the usual places yesterday.
    a. In NEUVILLE VITASSE.
    b. In trench at TELEGRAPH REDOUBT.
    c. In PINE TRENCH.
    d. In TELEGRAPH HILL TRENCH.
A fairly large working party was seen on NIGER TRENCH in N.16.d.
(5). General. There was a large party working somewhere on PINE LANE in the early morning. All sentries report a number of fires (probably cooking fires) along PINE LANE just before dawn. Smoke was seen rising from houses in the Eastern end of NEUVILLE VITASSE.
Two posts on TELEGRAPH HILL observed yesterday have disappeared.

HeadQrs. 56th Divn.
24th March, 1917.

General Staff.

War Diary

56th DIVISIONAL ARTILLERY.

Summary of Intelligence for 24 hours ending noon 24.3.17.

Aerial. Hostile aeroplanes encountered two of our machines when well over our lines at M.3.a.: in the air fight that ensued one of our 'planes fell in flames both pilot and observer being killed. This took place at 9.50 – 10 a.m.

Movement. 24.3.17. 7.3 a.m. 3 of the enemy proceeded from MILL at N.25.d.65.60. to look out post about N.25.d.40.45.m returning to the MILL shortly afterwards.

7.30 a.m. Enemy working in small parties in N.27.a.

General. 23.3.17. 1.15 p.m. Heavy artillery appeared to hit some inflammable material about N.19.b.6.8, large clouds of smoke rising.

24.3.17. 9.45 a.m. 2 balloons crossed our lines about 300 feet high to our South going S.W.

10.30 a.m. 1 balloon crossed our lines again dropping copies of the paper Gazette des Ardennes.

10.53 a.m. Balloon was seen close to ground in N.13.d. it rose and floated over our lines.

WANCOURT CHURCH has disappeared, it is thought as the result of an explosion observed at 4.15 p.m. yesterday.

REPORT on HOSTILE ARTILLERY FIRE.

Date & Time.	No. of Shell.	Nature.	Supposed position of Hostile Guns & how observed.	True Bearing of Flashes.	Position of Observer.	Locality Shelled.	Whether fire observed by aeroplane or balloon.
23.3.17. 3.30 p.m.	6	77 mm.	Due E. of BEAURAINS.	-	M.10.c.	Old "NO MAN'S LAND" in M.10.c.	
During night. 24.3.17.			Desultory scattered shelling of BEAURAINS and roads in vicinity.				
7.30—7.50 a.m.	12	77	E. of BEAURAINS	-	M.11.a.5.1.	Neighbourhood of O.P. at M.11.b. 15.20.	
8.10 am.	6	77	-	-	-	M.10.c.	

REPORT ON OUR ARTILLERY.

251st Bde Date & Time.	Batty. Firing	Nature of Gun.	No. of Shell. S.	No. of Shell. H.E.	Objective.	Report on effect of fire & quality of ammunition.	Remarks.
23.3.17. afternoon 9.a.pm. to	A.281	18-Pdr.	33	6	NEUVILLE VITASSE TRENCH.	Good.	Registration.
midnight 1 am. to	"	"	31	33	Roads in vicinity of N.19.b.75.85.		Night firing.
2.30 am.	109	"	35	30			
midnight to 3 a.m.	D.281	4.5"	-	66			
10.30 am. 250th 3de	B.281	18-Pdr.	31	26	Ruins of NEUVILLE VITASSE TRENCH	Fuzes not very regular.	Registration of in new position
Noon.							
4 p.m.	95	18-pdr.	40	40	N.13.d.; N.19.c. and N.19.a.		German working working party
12.30 pm.	C.280	"	12	-	NEUVILLE VITASSE		satisfactory
2.30 pm.	A.280	"	-	10	N.2.b.8.9.		Registration.
6.10 pm.	92	"	-	12			Working Party
8.0 p.m. to 5.30am	C.280	"	80	120	N.20.a.1.6.		Fork roads in re NEUVILLE VITASS

P.T.O.

SECRET.

War Diary

56th DIVISIONAL TACTICAL PROGRESS REPORT NO. 5
from 5 p.m. 24th March to 5 p.m. 25th March, 1917.

On receipt of current copy of Divisional Tactical Progress Report in the trenches, previous copy to be burnt.

PART I OPERATIONS.
BEAURAINS SECTION. (169th Inf.Bde.)
A. (1). Relief. The L.R.B. relieved the Q.W.R. in the Left Sub-section.
(2). Patrols. A patrol from the Q.W.R. proceeded along PREUSSEN REDOUBT as far as NICE TRENCH. On arrival at N.7.c.10.85 sounds of work were heard in TELEGRAPH REDOUBT. Two enemy patrols were seen in this neighbourhood.

A patrol from the Q.V.R. proceeded up VITASSE LANE for 200 yards above our post. Here the trench was filled in. Patrol then moved forward over the open in a N.E. direction. There is a small isolated post with a concrete emplacement, apparently for a M.G., and a store of stick grenades, a short way from the end of the trench. This was unoccupied. Patrol moved E for 100 yards when voices and work were heard. The officer advanced in the direction of the sounds for 50 yards when he was challenged, a flare was sent up and rifle and M.G. fire opened. One man was wounded. Our patrol withdrew carrying the casualty.

A patrol from the L.R.B. reconnoitred BATTERY Trench and TELEGRAPH LANE about M.12.d.7.8. 4 men were working on the wire at this point, but it could not be seen whether they were strengthening it or pulling it down. A party of about 30 was digging in the trench. A large white box with a padlock was found in the trench. It was not touched as a trap was suspected, but will be investigated further. The N.E. end of BATTERY TRENCH is organised as a fire trench, and has some dugouts intact.

(3). Artillery. Visibility fair.
Our guns were active against trenches on TELEGRAPH HILL and NEUVILLE VITASSE. Enemy working parties were seen and fired on at N.13.d., N.19.c. and a. and N.26.b.8.9.
(4). M.Gs. fired at hostile aeroplane.

PART II INTELLIGENCE.
BEAURAINS SECTION.
B. (1). Hostile Artillery. Fairly active throughout the day. Fire was directed on to our front line trenches and C.Ts. especially near the NEUVILLE VITASSE Road. Desultory fire all day and night in and around BEAURAINS. Most of the shells are 77 mm. and 4.2". A few 5.9" are reported.
(2). Hostile M.Gs. Fired frequent bursts all night along the NEUVILLE VITASSE Road from NEUVILLE VITASSE. Gun in TELEGRAPH HILL, fired in enfilade down our new front trench during the day.
(3). Hostile Patrols and Working Parties. See A. (1).
(4). Transport. Considerable noise is made by the enemy's transport behind NEUVILLE VITASSE every morning just before dawn. It was particularly noticeable this morning. Artillery of both sides is generally quiet at this time.
(5). Movement. None seen in NEUVILLE VITASSE. From 6 to 7 a.m. there was a good deal of movement on TELEGRAPH HILL. Men were seen digging in the trenches and one or two walked across the open from one trench to another. This movement can be seen from the rear end of PREUSSEN WEG but not from our forward posts.

The sunken road through N.7 central from TILLOY to NEUVILLE VITASSE is used considerably by the enemy. Movement of small parties is almost continuous, wagons and mounted men are seen from time to time. Single men and small parties were seen several times during the afternoon especially about the white chalk track in N.26 central, and on WANCOURT LINE about NIGER TRENCH (N.16 central)
(6). General. The trucks on the railway have been located at N.14.a. 5.2. Aeroplanes were active. One of ours was brought down over the German lines at 7 a.m. Hostile balloon ascended late in the afternoon for about 45 mins. (T.B from M.10.c.45.15 gives 57°).

Head Qrs. 56th Divn.
26th March, 1917.

for Lieut-Colonel
General Staff.

P.2. T.P.R.No.5.

REPORT ON OUR ARTILLERY. (Contd.)
From 12 noon 25.3.17 to 12 noon 26.3.17.

281st Bde.

Date & Time.	Battery Firing.	Nature of Gun.	No. of S.	Shell H.E.	Objective.	Observation employed.	Report on effect of fire & quality of ammtn.	Remarks.
25.3.17. 2.15 pm. to 4.45. do.	A/281 " "	18 pdr. " "	20 100 108	" " "	N.19.a.25.75 do. do.		Good. " Fuzes bursting irregularly.	Registration of wire. Firing for effect. Lanes partially cut through the wire.
3.30 p.m.	D/281	4.5" How.	-	47	Active Hostile Battery N.21.c.2.9.	Unobserved.		Unobserved.
5.15 to 5.15 pm.	B/29h	18 pdr.	160	-	N.13.c.5.5.		Satisfactory.	Lane partially cut through wire at this point.
26.3.17. 12 midnight onward. During night.	A/281 B/281	" "	100 60	- -	Lane in wire at N.19.a.25. 75. " " " N.13.c.5.5.		- -	Keeping same open. " " "
Midnight to 5.0 a.m.	D/281	4.5" How.	90	-	Roads and tracks in area of NEUVILLE VITASSE.		-	Night firing.

REPORT ON ACTION OF 281 Bde. 56th D.A. for 24 hours ending 10 a.m. 25.3.17.

Position & A.H.No. of Hostile Battery engaged for effect.

Approximate co-ordinates of wire cut.

3.40 p.m. 25th inst. at   Unobserved.   (a). N.19.a.25.75.
E.21.c.2.9. Active   (b). N.13.c.5.5.
Hostile battery reported   Lanes were partially cut but wire is
47 Rds. 4.5" How.   deep and in the case (b) is in four
                                                        belts.

T.P.R.No.5.

REPORT ON HOSTILE ARTILLERY.
From 12 noon 25.3.17 to 12 noon 26.3.17.

Date & Time.	Number & Nature of shell.	Supposed position of hostile guns and how obtained. F. G. S.	True bearing of flashes.	Position of observer.	Locality shelled.	Whether fire was directed by aeroplane or balloon.
25.3.17 Noon to 5.30 p.m.	Many H.E. about 200 mostly 4.2" some 5.9"	—			M.16.a.	M.18.& M.24.a. Our new trenches here.
3.30 to 4.30 p.m.	25 5.9"	—			M.10.c.	About M.3.d.95.30.
6.30 p.m.	6. 21 cm.H.E.	—				M.17.a.
25.3.17. Nature. 3.0 p.m. 25Ax 4.2"How					Battery Position M.10.a.15.20	M.10.a.
12 noon to 12.30 pm. 12Ax 77 mm.					Battery Pos. M.10.c.43.32	JAGER WEG.
5.30 pm. to 6.30pm. 30Ax 4.2"How 8.45 pm. 10Ax 5.9"	) Direction WANCOURT (S))				)Battery Pos.)M.10.c.45.15	PREUSSEN WEG S.E.BEAURAINS	Balloon was up between 6 & 6.30 p.m. on T.B.of 570 from M.10.c. 45.15.

Intermittent 77 mm. & 4.2" Shrapnel on TRACKS during the whole night Direction WANCOURT (S).

REPORT on OUR ARTILLERY.
From 12 Noon 25.3.17 to 12 noon 26.3.17.

280th Bde.

Date & Time.	Nature of gun.	Battery firing.	Number of shell. S. H.E.	Objective.	Report on effect of fire and quality of ammunition.	Remarks.
25.3.17 12 noon to 2 pm	18 pdr.	93rd	30. 20.	N.25.b. & N.14.a.		
4.30 pm.to 6.30	"	"	200	about M.24.b.8.3.	Satisfactory.	Sniping at Hermans here.
7.30pm.to 9 pm.	4.5"How.	D/280	— 40 BX.—)			Wire-cutting - Group Order.
9 pm. to 11 pm.	18 pdr.	C/280	15 35)	N.20.a.10.65.		
25th 5am.to 6 am.	"	C/280	15 35)			Cross Roads here. GROUP PROGRAMME.
10.15 a.m.	"	A/280	2 —	NEUVILLE MILL		2 Germans seen here.

P.T.O.

SECRET.

War Diary Copy

56th DIVISIONAL TACTICAL PROGRESS REPORT No. 4.
from 5.0 p.m. 23rd March to 5.0 p.m. 24th March, 1917.

On receipt of current copy of Divisional Tactical Progress Report in the trenches, previous copy to be burnt.

PART I OPERATIONS.
    BEAURAINS SECTION (169th Inf.Bde.)
      (a). Patrols. The PREUSSEN REDOUBT was patrolled from M.18.b.25.80 in a North Easterly direction to M.12.d.8.5. No signs of the enemy were found.
      (b). Artillery. Our Artillery was active during the day shelling TELEGRAPH HILL and NEUVILLE VITASSE.
      (c). General. Posts were established at M.18.d.6.3. and M.18.b.8.2.

PART II INTELLIGENCE.
    BEAURAINS SECTION. (169th Inf.Bde.)
      (b). Hostile Artillery. During the night the Southern end of the PREUSSEN WEG and our front line trenches in M.18. central were shelled with 77 mm guns and 4.2 in. hows.
    During the day our posts in front of the right subsector were lightly shelled with shrapnel, and the front line with 5.9 inch.
      (c). Hostile Machine Guns. A M.G. emplacement is suspected at N.7.c.1.7. Flashes were seen from this neighbourhood during the night. Two men looked over the parapet here during the day and later a gun appeared to fire at one of our aeroplanes from this spot.
    Another emplacement is suspected at N.14.c.2.4.
    A M.G. fired down the NEUVILLE VITASSE - BEAURAINS road intermittently during the night, and the MERCATEL road was sprayed from the direction of NEUVILLE VITASSE.
      (d). Hostile Patrols. At 5.15 a.m. a hostile patrol, 6 or 7 strong approached our post at M.18.d.6.3. Rapid fire was opened and the patrol retired.
      (e). Hostile Working Parties. From 5.40 to 9.40 a.m. a party of 10 men appeared to be collecting planks from about N.14.c.2.4., carrying them along the road to about N.8.d.80.75.
      (f). Hostile Movement. Considerable movement was observed during the day. Parties are reported using the Sunken Road in N.13.b. & d. and also along the road from NEUVILLE VITASSE through N.14.a. At 10.30 a.m. 3 parties of about 25 men followed by some horsemen proceeded along the road from NEUVILLE VITASSE towards TILLOY.
    At dawn 2 parties each of 3 men walked from NEUVILLE VITASSE to PINE TRENCH. At 7 a.m. two men looked over the parapet in LEAF TRENCH at N.19.a.0.6.
    At 12.30 p.m. one man in a light blue uniform walked into NEUVILLE VITASSE from TELEGRAPH HILL TRENCH.
    A party of 5 men entered the trench at N.34.b.05.40.
    A man appeared to be working a windlass at N.34.a.9.4.
    A party of horsemen rode along the road in N.25.b.
      (g). Hostile Transport. A G.S. wagon was observed on the road in N.35.b. Three wagons loaded with timber were observed to arrive behind TELEGRAPH HILL. Transport was heard behind NEUVILLE VITASSE at 5.10 a.m.
      (h). General. Between 10.30 and 11 a.m. four small balloons rose from the German Trenches. These blew over ACHICOURT and ARRAS and appeared to drop papers.
    There appears to be a dump at N.13.b.6.4.
    Smoke was seen throughout the day in FERN TRENCH about N.13.d.25.20.

Head Qrs. 56th Divn.
25th March, 1917.   P.T.O.

for Lt. Col.
General Staff.

T.P.R.No.4.

REPORT ON HOSTILE ARTILLERY FIRE.
From 12 noon 24.3.17 to 12 noon 25.3.17.

Date & Time.	Number and Nature of Shell.	Supposed position of hostile guns & how obtained. F. S. G.	True bearing of flashes.	Position of Observer	Locality shelled.	Whether fire was directed by aeroplane or balloon.
Noon.	15 H.E.5.9" How.	-	-	AGNY.	AGNY	Suggested result of hostile Air Reconnaissance.
1 p.m.	5 H.E.4.2" "	-	-	M.10.c.	M.10.c.	
3 p.m.	4 4.2" Gun.	-	-	-	M.11.c.	
3.15 p						
4 p.m.	20 77 m/m	N.2.b.	-	-	Road M.15.c.	
4.50 pm.	15 77 m/m	N.2.b.	-	-	M.15.c.	
6.20 pm.	5 4.2" How.	-	-	-	M.13.a.5.7.	
6.50 pm.	10 77 m/m	N.2.b.	-	-	M.16.a.5.7.	
7 - 8 pm.	200 4.2" How.	Left of MONCHY.	-	-	M.10.c.	by map.

SUMMARY OF INTELLIGENCE.

Considerable Aerial activity during the day, several of our planes being engaged by enemy machines. German working parties were engaged at various times by 18 pdr. Batteries in N.13., N.15., N.25 and N.27. Hostile Artillery exploded a small ammunition dump during the evening about M.10.a.

REPORT OF OUR ARTILLERY.

280th Brigade.

Date & Time.	Nature of gun.	Battery firing	Number of shell. S.	H.E.	Objective.	Report on effect of fire & quality of ammunition	Remarks.
24.3.17 - 25.3.17.							
1 p.m. - 1.35pm.	18 pdr.	93rd	30	15	N.13.a. & b.	Satisfactory.	Small parties of Germans on tracks here.
1.20 p.m.	"	A/280	6	-	N.13.d.55.30.	"	3 Germans crossing road at trench here.
1.45 - 2.30 pm.	"	93rd	35	20	N.13.c. & d.	"	Registration of trenches h
3.5 p.m.	"	A/280	4	4	N.15.b.	"	Small German party in the open.
3.15-5 pm.	"	93rd	20	10	N.26.b. & 27.a.	"	Sniping Germans crossing crest here.
8.30pm-5 am.	"	A/280	80	120	N.20.a.1.6.	"	Fork Road.Night Programme
4.15 p.m.	"	93rd	4	4	N.13.a.	"	Movement seen here.

War Diary

SECRET.

56th DIVISIONAL TACTICAL PROGRESS REPORT No.6
from 5.0 p.m. 25th March to 5.0 p.m. 26th March 1917.

On receipt of current copy of Divisional Tactical Progress Report in the trenches, previous copy to be burnt.

PART I OPERATIONS.
BEAURAINS SECTION. (169th Inf.Bde.)
(1). Our patrols were inactive owing to covering parties being out in front of Brigades on our flanks, and our own covering party along DEODAR LANE N. of the NEUVILLE VITASSE Road.
(2). Artillery. Usual firing on to NEUVILLE-VITASSE and TELEGRAPH HILL. Satisfactory progress was made during the day in cutting lane in wire at N.19.a.25.75. Wire cutting group programme was carried out from 11 a.m. to noon on M.24.d.75.85. Also fired at movement throughout the day. Visibility fair.
(3). M.Gs. fired at hostile aircraft.

PART II INTELLIGENCE.
BEAURAINS SECTION.
(1). Hostile artillery. Very active between 11 p.m. and 4 p.m. mostly against trenches about M.18 central. 8 4.2's were fired at 2.0 p.m. on to M.10.c. BEAURAINS was shelled during the day with 40 4.2's. Hostile artillery also fired on to NEUVILLE POST.
(2). Hostile M.Gs. Active all night against usual targets.
(3). Hostile Trench Mortars. A medium T.M. fired on to posts in PREUSSEN REDOUBT during the night. Location about N.13.a.3.8. 4.5" Hows. replied promptly
(4). Hostile Patrols. A party of 20 to 30 of the enemy attempted to raid our post at M.18.b.20.85. They threw several bombs into the post wounding 3 men but were driven off by Lewis Gun and rifle fire. Enemy working parties were fired on during the day in N.14.a. and c., N.19.d. and were dispersed in all cases.
(5). Movement. Observation very poor all day and very little movement was seen

Single men and small parties seen on distant crests E. of NEUVILLE & S.E. of WANCOURT, parties were too far away to be dealt with. During the night patrols reported enemy working parties at junction of NEUFCHATEL LANE and PINE LANE. The gaps at N.13.c.5.5. and N.19.a.25.75 in the intervals of M.G.fire were being worked on.

At 11.15 a.m., 27th. abnormal activity was seen on the COJEUL Line in N.20.d., 26.b., 21.c. and 27.a. - also on back crests small scattered parties being at work.
(6). Transport. Was heard between 9 and 10 p.m. as well as in early morning behind NEUVILLE VITASSE.
(7). General. The enemy was using a searchlight behind TELEGRAPH HILL during the night.

At 6 p.m. two of our aeroplanes flying very low over the trenches on TELEGRAPH HILL, were not fired on by M.Gs. as is usually done.

Head Qrs. 56th Divn.
27th March, 1917.

Intelligence, General Staff.

56th DIVISIONAL TACTICAL PROGRESS REPORT No. 7.
From 5.0 p.m. 26th March to 5.0 p.m. 27th March 1917.

On receipt of current copy of Divisional Tactical Progress Report in the trenches, previous copy to be burnt.

PART I OPERATIONS.

BEAURAINS SECTION. (169th Inf.Bde.)

(1). <u>Patrols</u>. From the 2nd London Regt.

A patrol under an officer proceeded up NEUVILLE LANE. When about 30 yards forward of the junction with DEODAR LANE they were fired on by a M.G. After waiting some time they advanced another 50 yards when enemy M.G. again opened fire and patrol withdrew.

From the L.R.B.

A strong patrol under an officer moved up NEUFCHATEL LANE. When 100 yards from PINE LANE sounds of work were heard. The officer and 2 men advanced and saw a large party. Men could be seen moving in the wire at N.13.c.5.5. apparently repairing damage done to wire by our artillery. Sounds were heard of a large party digging in PINE LANE at junction with NEUFCHATEL LANE, and also further to the right. Patrol moved 150 yards to the right and found that enemy were working on the wire about N.19.a.25.75 and that digging was in progress all along PINE LANE to the right. Our artillery were informed.

Another officers' patrol went out at 9 p.m. from BATTERY TRENCH, went N.E. over two tracks to TELEGRAPH LANE. The latter was unoccupied. The trench is 3 to 4 feet deep, no revetting or duckboards and did not look as if it had ever been occupied. Patrol crossed the trench and saw a post of 2 men in some mounds, believed to be COPSE TRENCH. Patrol moved to the enemy's right and a second sentry post was seen. A M.G. was firing from the HARP but could not be definitely located. Several green flares were fired grom N.W. of TELEGRAPH HILL.

(2). <u>Artillery</u>. Our artillery were engaged in wire cutting. Gaps were cut at N.19.a.25.75., N.13.c.5.5., M.24.d.75.87. These points were fired on during the night to prevent repairs being made. We also shelled the roads in rear of NEUVILLE VITASSE.

(3). <u>Machine Guns</u>. Fired at smoke in valley behind TELEGRAPH HILL and men walking about near it.

PART II INTELLIGENCE.   Visibility fair.

BEAURAINS SECTION.

(1) <u>Hostile Artillery</u>. Active on to the BEAURAINS-MERCATEL Road between 5.30 and 6.15 a.m. 77 mm. shells fell on to JACKMANN STELLUNG and DEODAR LANE between midday and 2 p.m.

(2). <u>Hostile M.Gs</u>. Active during night and early morning against usual targets.

(3). <u>Hostile Patrols</u>. None encountered.

(4). <u>Movement</u>. Working and carrying parties were seen in the neighbourhood of WANCOURT and HENINEL. Small working parties were seen on NEPAL TRENCH in N.21.d. and around the EGG in N.20.d. Usual Movement on TELEGRAPH HILL at dawn.

27.3.17. Considerable movement and new workings on the WANCOURT LINE in N.27.a. & c. and on trench in N.34.b. & d. Numerous small parties seen on back crests and parties of two or three between WANCOURT & NEUVILLE VITASSE. White smoke seen during the afternoon issuing from about N.14. - 4 men observed walking away from neighbourhood. Fire burning most of the day in square N.8. Dugouts or old gun positions were seen to be smoking all day at N.13.b.40.10. Movement is continually seen around the O.P. at N.25.d.26.51.

General. Considerable quantities of smoke were seen at intervals of 30 yds. along road in N.8.c. There were 3 columns and the flames from one were about 6 feet high. During shelling of NEUVILLE VITASSE 6 white flares were sent up from S.E. corner of the village. These were followed by 6 from BOIRY COPSE or thereabout, then 10 more from the same place in NEUVILLE VITASSE. Four Very Lights were fired at 4.25 pm by the enemy in N.25.d. No resulting action.

Head Qrs. 56th Divn.
28th March, 1917.

T.C.Hreld A.
Intelligence, General Staff.

SECRET.

War Diary

56th DIVISIONAL TACTICAL PROGRESS REPORT No. 8.
from 5.0 p.m. 27th March to 5.0 p.m. 28th March 1917.

On receipt of current copy of Divisional Tactical Progress Report in the trenches, previous copy to be burnt.

PART I OPERATIONS.
BEAURAINS SECTION (169th Inf.Bde.)

Patrols. An Officer and 10 O.Rs. reconnoitred VITASSE LANE. On reaching M.24.b.85.35 an enemy party was heard at approximately M.19.a.14.29. Our patrol opened fire and the enemy dispersed. Our patrol returned and reported VITASSE LANE unoccupied but NEUVILLE VITASSE held by the enemy.

A small patrol under an N.C.O. went out to investigate gap in the enemy wire at N.19.a.25.75. A large party of the enemy were working at this point. Patrol was fired on by M.G. Casualties nil.

A small patrol went out to ascertain if gap at M.24.b.8.3. was still open. A party of the enemy were found working on the wire.

Two officers carried out a reconnaissance of NEUVILLE and VITASSE LANES at midday. They found that VITASSE LANE was filled in from M.24.b.7.5. S.E. as far as they could see, and that NEUVILLE LANE was filled in from M.24.b.5.3. S.E. for 40 yards.

A patrol examined the enemy's wire from N.13.c.6.4. to N.13.c.7.6. but could find no signs of a gap.

Our artillery continued their wire cutting programme at following points (a) M.19.a.60.88. (b) N.13.c.5.5. lane now cut (c) N.13.c.50.90. (d) N.19.a.25.70 Lane appears to be clear. We shelled NEUVILLE VITASSE and enemy tracks at "dawn". On receiving a message from the infantry patrols that the enemy were working on the gaps in their wire, fire was opened and continued at intervals throughout the night.

PART II INTELLIGENCE. Observation was poor yesterday.
BEAURAINS SECTION.

Hostile Artillery shelled AGNY, ACHICOURT & BEAURAINS during the afternoon and evening. One of our batteries was also shelled and a small ammunition dump hit.

Hostile Machine Guns. Usual fire from TELEGRAPH HILL and NEUVILLE VITASSE. Gun located at approximately M.12.b.5.5.

Hostile Movement. 6-7 a.m. Parties of 4 men seen walking from N. of NEUVILLE VITASSE to PINE LANE.

12 noon. Officers at M.24.b.8.4. saw considerable movement in N.13.c. and d.

Small quantities of smoke were coming from suspected old hostile gun pits in N.8.c.

A digging and carrying party of 12 men was seen at N.34.b.1.2.

A party of about 10 men working on trench about N.27.a.4.7. continuously throughout the day.

A party of 10 men, a horse and cart, and a pair horse limber, were seen on Road in N.30.b.

Thirty men seen on road at N.17.d.6.2. proceeding towards WANCOURT.

Two fires were seen during the afternoon in WANCOURT.

Two parties of 12 men each were seen working on the top of ridge in N.29.b. and N.30.a.

General. Muffled explosions were heard in NEUVILLE VITASSE at 7.15 a.m. and smoke was seen to rise from a point about N.19.a.1.2.

An enemy sniper fired at movement in PREUSSEN REDOUBT TRENCHES. His position appeared to be about M.19.a.1.2. Aircraft very active. One of our planes was seen to come down low and fire into the enemy's trenches.

Eight hostile observation balloons were visible.

Head Qrs. 56th Divn.
29th March, 1917.

F.C.Hrald
Lieutenant,
Intelligence, General Staff.

War Diary

SECRET.

**56th DIVISIONAL TACTICAL PROGRESS REPORT No.9
from 5 p.m. 28th March to 5 p.m. 29th March 1917.**

On receipt of current copy of Divisional Tactical Progress Report in the trenches, previous copy to be burnt.

PART I OPERATIONS.
BEAURAINS SECTION (169th Inf.Bde.)

Patrols. An N.C.O. and 4 men reconnoitred place where artillery had been cutting wire at N.19.a.25.75. They went along the BEAURAINS - NEUVILLE VITASSE Road to the Bank at M.18.d.7.2. From this point they pushed on until close up to LEAF TRENCH at N.19.a.25.75. No wire could be found at this point, but a number of stakes were seen. Patrol was unable to proceed further owing to our own artillery fire. Whilst this patrol was out 3 explosions were heard by them in NEUVILLE VITASSE.

A patrol went out to examine gap cut by our artillery in wire at M.24.b.8.3. A large enemy party with three covering parties was discovered at work in NEUVILLE WORK. Our artillery dealt with them.

A patrol went out to NEUVILLE VITASSE to discover if the enemy were still there in strength. On approaching within 25 yards of trench running through N.19.a.1.2. voices and digging were heard in the trench. The officer and 2 O.Rs. attempted to get nearer but were challenged at once, bombs were thrown, and rifle and M.G. fire was opened. Our patrol replied with rifle fire, but as the enemy's fire increased our patrol withdrew. The enemy sent up flares and his 77 mm. guns opened fire promptly.

A strong patrol of an officer and 25 men proceeded up NEUFCHATEL LANE towards NEUVILLE VITASSE to find out whether the Germans were still holding the village in strength. Patrol halted about 20 yards in front of PINE LANE and the officer and 4 men went up to the enemy's wire. Sentry was seen and heard in PINE LANE, N. of NEUFCHATEL LANE. South of NEUFCHATEL Lane sentries were seen every 10 yards. There was no gap in wire, but there is a track along outside of wire which suggested that it is patrolled regularly. Several telephone wires were found running towards our lines all of which were cut. Work was heard along PINE LANE to the North.

Artillery. Our guns very active during the afternoon. Several rounds fired into NEUVILLE VITASSE which did not explode. At 3.40 a.m. one shell fell 2 yards in front of our post on the BEAURAINS - NEUVILLE VITASSE Road. It did not explode but showered earth over the garrison. Our artillery continued the wire cutting programmes. A lane 18 yds. in width was cut at M.24.b.85.05 and commenced at N.19.a.60.88. Patrols report that the enemy had repaired gaps at N.13.c.5.5., N.13.c.5.9. and N.19.a.25.75. Fire could only be maintained on these gaps for two hours during the night owing to our patrols being out. Registration was carried out on points in NEUVILLE VITASSE.

PART II INTELLIGENCE.
Visibility intermittent owing to rain.
BEAURAINS SECTION. -
Hostile Artillery were active. BEAURAINS was shelled with 5.9" & 4.2" in the evening. Our roads and tracks were shrapnelled during the night, and PREUSSEN WEG was shelled with 77 mm. in the early morning.
Also
Hostile M.Gs. were active from NEUVILLE VITASSE during the night. fired on our patrol. The TELEGRAPH HILL gun did not fire.

Hostile Movement. At 12 noon three parties each of 6 to 10 men were observed to leave the S.E. portion of NEUVILLE VITASSE and disappear over ridge S.W. of the village. A party of 5 men were seen in the morning coming from behind NEUVILLE VITASSE. An 18 pdr. shell burst near them and they scattered at the double.

Movement was seen during the day on the TILLOY WANCOURT Road.

A good deal of movement was seen on CAMBRAI Road near FEUCHY CHAPEL and in HINDENBURG LINE in N.7.d. A party of 12 men was seen digging in trench at N.13.a.55.95. 5 men seen in trench at N.14.c.10.55. 3 men appeared to be examining trench at N.13.b.8.8. Usual working parties were seen round WANCOURT and on NEPAL TRENCH and NEUVILLE VITASSE TRENCH.

General. Enemy used flares for the first time from NEUVILLE VITASSE last night. A small enemy field gun is suspected to fire from some part of NEUVILLE VITASSE or just outside the S.E. part of the Village.

Head Qrs. 56th Divn. 30.3.17.

T.C.Heald. Lieut
Intelligence, General Staff.

War Diary

SECRET.

56th DIVISIONAL TACTICAL PROGRESS REPORT No.10.
from 5 p.m. 29th March to 5 p.m. 30th March 1917.

On receipt of current copy of Divisional Tactical Progress Report in the trenches, previous copy to be burnt.

PART I OPERATIONS.

BEAURAINS SECTION (169th Inf.Bde.)

Our Artillery continued their wire-cutting programme, points fired at being N.13.c.5.9., N.19.a.60.88 - wire much damaged - M.24.b. 80.30. These points were kept under fire during the night to prevent repair. The cross roads at N.20.a.05.65., N.20.b.65.78 and N.20.c.45.70. were also shelled during the night.

At 8.30 p.m. an Officers' patrol left our trenches at M.18.b.6.3. and worked Northwards along DEODAR LANE. The trench has been filled in from 200 yards North of this point to about M.12.d.8.1. The trench from DEODAR LANE to M.18.b.6.9. and that to the Sunken Road at N.7.c.0.1. have both been filled in. The wire in front of the Sunken Road in M.12.d.is reported 8 feet wide and 3 feet high. The patrol then moved West to BONE TRENCH at M.12.d.70.05, where the trench was partly filled in. A hostile working party estimated at 20 strong was observed working about M.12.d.6.2. Subsequently this party was dispersed by artillery fire.

A patrol reconnoitred NEUFCHATEL LANE as far as the German wire at N.13.c.5.4. The wire from here to the North for 400 yards has no gaps. At N.13.c.5.9. considerable repairs have been done on the wire. Talking was heard along the whole of this part of PINE LANE. The gun pits at N.13.c.35.80 were unoccupied.

An Officers' patrol left our trenches at 5.20 a.m. and advanced towards NEUVILLE VITASSE keeping about 30 yards to the South of the BEAURAINS Road. A few strands of wire were encountered in a dip in the ground at about M.24.b.80.75. Our patrol cut this wire and moved forward until talking was heard from the Village. The Officer and part of the patrol then moved forward to within view of the trench that joins the road at N.19.a.2.4. From the noise and talking heard it was evident that this trench was strongly held.

A patrol reconnoitred the German wire in M.24.d. Only one gap was discovered, this being a clear lane through the wire 12 feet wide at M.24.d.7.9., where there are wheel tracks. The wire on either side of the gap is 20 yards deep.

A patrol sent out to reconnoitre gaps at N.19.a.25.75 failed to locate the gap, but a small trench filled with brushwood and hurdles was located running from approximately N.19.a.05.75. to N.19.a.25.80.

PART II INTELLIGENCE.

BEAURAINS SECTION.- Hostile Artillery showed considerable activity, especially between 4 and 5 p.m. and during the night. The roads and tracks in and around BEAURAINS were shelled during the day, and shrapnel and light H.E. shells were indiscriminately fired on to our trenches during the day and night, mostly falling near the S. end of PREUSSEN WEG.

A hostile M.G. was located by one of our patrols firing from about M.12.d.95.30. The usual intermittent bursts were fired during the night on the BEAURAINS - NEUVILLE VITASSE Road.

Hostile Working Parties. 20 Germans located working at M.12.d.6.2. The enemy were seen working on TELEGRAPH HILL at dawn: the point where they were working was subsequently bombarded by our Artillery.

Hostile Movement. During the day a wagon and several small parties of men were seen on the TILLOY - WANCOURT Road. Movement was observed on TELEGRAPH HILL. Men were seen carrying timber in FERN Tr. 3 small parties of men observed moving S.E. on the road at N.14.a.8.8. Smoke was seen N.E. of NEUVILLE VITASSE. Considerable movement observed round huts at N.29.d.9.7., also men were loading trucks at this point.

8 men seen on road in N.30.a. and N.30.b. moving East.

T.F.C.Hjalda Lieut
Intelligence, General Staff.

Head Qrs. 56th Divn.
31st March, 1917.

SECRET.   *War Diary*

56th DIVISIONAL TACTICAL PROGRESS REPORT No. 11
from 5 p.m. 30th March to 5 p.m. 31st March, 1917.

On receipt of current copy of Divisional Tactical Progress Report in the trenches, previous copy to be burnt.

PART I OPERATIONS.
BEAURAINS SECTION. (169th Inf.Bde.)

Patrols. No patrols were sent out last night in order that artillery might keep gaps open in the enemy's wire.

Our artillery continued their wire cutting yesterday. Points fired at being N.19.a.60.88. N.13.c.5.9. Partial lane cut N.13.c.5.5. M.24.d.75.87. M.24.d.75.70. N.19.c.20.35. These were kept under fire throughout the night to prevent repairs being made. We also fired on roads in rear of NEUVILLE VITASSE at movement seen.

PART II INTELLIGENCE.   Visibility - Good at times.
BEAURAINS SECTION. - Hostile Artillery.
Slightly more active than usual. PREUSSEN WEG, ASH TRENCH and FALLOW TRENCH were shelled frequently during the night with 7.7. cm. DEODAR LANE also shelled at night. BEAURAINS and roads fired on at intervals as usual.

Hostile M.Gs. Usual night firing from TELEGRAPH HILL and NEUVILLE VITASSE.

Movement. 5.30 p.m. 10 men marching in single file at N.8.c.5.8. 6 men walking in the open at N.14.c.15.40, dispersed by a round of shrapnel.

Light railway along road in N.29.d. and N.30.c. was used considerably.

A large enemy party about 100 strong was seen working at approximately N.14.a.3.5. (THE ARK) from 5 a.m. to 8 a.m. Men were seen to be carrying shovels.

Two men seen to enter tower at N.24.d.1.0. One man carried a shining object on his shoulder. Shortly afterwards something was seen glinting from the top of the tower.

Movement was seen in Gunpits at N.13.b.4.0.

Almost continuous movement of small parties along TILLOY WANCOURT Road.

A great many working parties and small bodies of men were observed on the ridges in back areas.

Enemy were seen at work on COJEUL SWITCH at several points.

3.30 p.m. 3 Germans seen coming over open from N.8.c. carrying rifles entered trench at N.7.d.

General. Flares were sent up from NEUVILLE VITASSE, apparently from N.19.a.1.2.

From 10 to 11 a.m. smoke was seen rising from the ground at N.19.b.45.60.

3.15 p.m. a large periscope was seen at N.13.d.6.3. for 20 minutes. The sun was shining on the glass.

Intelligence, General Staff.

Head Qrs. 56th Divn.
1st April, 1917.

SECRET.　　　　　　　　　　　　　　　　56th Divn. G.A.75.

167th Infantry Brigade.	56th Div. Train.
168th Infantry Brigade.	Div. M.G. Officer.
169th Infantry Brigade.	Div. Gas Officer.
C.R.A.	D.A.D.O.S.
C.R.E.	4th Aust. Div. Supply Column.
1/5th Cheshire Regt.	No. 2 Ammn. Sub Park.
A.D.M.S.	G.O.C.
"Q"	A.D.C.
A.P.M.	War Diary.
193rd Div. M.G. Coy.	File.
56th Div. Signals.	

The 50th Divisional Artillery is being detached temporarily to the VII Corps.

2.　　It will move on the 29th March, 1917, from OUTREBOIS via DOULLENS and LUCHEUX to HUMEERCOURT and COULLEMONT. H.Qrs. COUTURELLE.

3.　　On 30th instant it will move via main DOULLENS - ARRAS ROAD and BAC du SUD to WAILLY.

4.　　On arrival the 50th Divisional Artillery will be grouped with the 56th Divisional Artillery.

5.　　Supply Railhead WARLINCOURT, 30th March.

6.　　ACKNOWLEDGE.

Head Qrs. 56th Divn.　　　　　　　　　　　Lieut-Colonel,
27th March, 1917.　　　　　　　　　　　　General Staff.

SECRET.   56th Div. No.G.A.60

56th DIVISION INSTRUCTIONS.
MEDICAL ARRANGEMENTS

Bearers. 1. Head Qrs. of O.C., Bearers, will be at the dugout (Advanced Bearer Post) M.4.c.15.70., near the cross roads.

2. 8 bearers will be attached by A.D.M.S. to each Infantry Battalion on Z - 1 day.

3. A further Advanced Bearer Post is in cellars at BEAURAINS at M.4.d.65.00.

Further advanced posts will be established as necessity arises.

4. Battalion Medical Officers requiring further bearer assistance will communicate in writing to Officer i/c nearest Advanced Bearer Post, stating the actual number of lying cases.

Divisional Advanced Dressing Station.

The Divisional A.D.S. has been established at ACHICOURT - M.2.b.40.95., to which all lying cases will be taken.

Walking Cases will proceed by tracks, to be marked out under the orders of the A.D.M.S., to the Corps Wounded Walking Collecting Post at AGNY

B. Pakenham
Lieut-Colonel,
General Staff.

Head Qrs. 56th Divn.
28th March, 1917.

Copies to -
167th Inf.Bde.
168th Inf.Bde.
169th Inf.Bde.
VII Corps
" "   Arty.
" "   H.A.
C.R.A.
C.R.E.
1/5th Cheshire Regt.
A.D.M.S.
"Q"
A.P.M.

193rd Div.M.G.Coy.
56th Div.Signals.
56th Div.Train.
Div.M.G.Officer.
Div.Gas Officer.
D.A.D.O.S.
4th Aust.Div.Supply Col.
No.2 Ammn.Sub Park.
G.O.C.
A.D.C.
War Diary.
File.

SECRET.   56th Divn. No.G.A.85.

56th DIVISION INSTRUCTIONS.

ACTION OF MASSED MACHINE GUNS.

1. __169th Bde. M.G.Coy.__

    Will provide 8 guns to be placed near M.23.b.7.6. under the orders of the Divisional M.G.Officer.

    __Objective.__ - to fire on the hostile positions from TELEGRAPH WORK in N.7.a. down the COJEUL SWITCH to N.14.c. and also on NEUVILLE VITASSE, covering the advance of the infantry by overhead fire.

    On the occupation of the BLUE LINE by us, these guns will advance to a position in M.24.d. (about the 90 contour line) and assist the attack on the BROWN LINE.

    __Ammunition Dumps.__ - will be formed at M.23.b.7.6.

    __Remainder of Company__ will be with 169th Infantry Brigade in Divisional Reserve.

2. __193rd (Div.) M.G.Coy.__

    Will provide 8 guns, which will be echelonned by the Divisional M.G.Officer as follows :-

    (a) 2 guns about M.11.d.5.9.

    (b) 2 guns in BATTERY TRENCH about M.12.c.85.10.

    (c) 4 guns to assemble as far forward as possible, and, as soon as the attack on the BLUE LINE has been launched, to select positions on the left flank from which to bring fire to bear in a Northerly or North Easterly direction.

    __Object.__   To prevent attacks from the North or North East, and in the event of non-success by the Division on our left, to aid in the formation of a defensive flank by means of cross fire.

    __Ammunition Dumps.__ - near positions (a) & (b) & the site selected for (c).

    __Remainder of Company.__ - will be in Divisional Reserve, with its pack

P.T.O.

pack animals, and be ready to move forward quickly as may be required.

3. Co-operation with 30th Division.

30th Division is prepared to provide 8 machine guns about M.30 central to fire into NEUVILLE VITASSE and along the valley South of it until Zero + 2 hours, with the object of keeping the enemy below ground, of preventing reinforcements entering the Village from the S.E., and of causing loss on any enemy driven from the Village.

When the 30th Division has occupied the BLUE LINE these guns are to fire down the valley towards N.20.d. until masked by their own infantry, when they are to be brought into positions which will afford protection to the right flank of 56th Division.

56th Division.

When the capture of NEUVILLE VITASSE has been effected, the Divisional M.G.Officer will arrange to bring forward 8 guns to a position about the N.E. end of the 90 contour line in N.19 from which to bring fire to bear on NEUVILLE VITASSE TRENCH and assist the advance of 30th Division.

B Pakenham
Lieut-Colonel,
General Staff.

Head Qrs. 56th Divn.
29th March, 1917.

Copies to -
  167th Inf. Bde.
  168th Inf. Bde.
  169th Inf. Bde.
  VII Corps.
  " " Arty.
  " " H.A.
  C.R.A.
  C.R.E.
  1/5th Cheshire Regt.
  A.D.M.S.
  "Q"
  A.P.M.

193rd Div. M.G.Coy.
56th Div. Signals.
56th Div. Train.
Div. M.G.Officer.
Div. Gas Officer.
D.A.D.O.S.
4th Aust. Div. Supply Column.
No. 2 Ammn. Sub Park.
G.O.C.
A.D.C.
War Diary.
File.

SECRET.   Copy No. 23

56th DIVISION INSTRUCTIONS.

ASSEMBLY AREAS & ALLOTMENT OF TRENCHES FOR TRAFFIC.

1. Assembly Areas of the two Assaulting and the Reserve Brigades are shown on the attached Sketch Map.

2. On this map is shown the R.A.M.C. Area.

3. In the Reserve Brigade Area accommodation will be allotted for :-

    3 Coys. 1/5th Cheshire Regiment.
    2 Field Coys. R.E.
    2 Sections 193rd M.G.Coy.

4. ACKNOWLEDGE.

B Pakenham
Lieut-Colonel,
General Staff.

Head Qrs. 56th Divn.
30th March, 1917.

Copy No. 1. 167th Inf. Bde.   13. 193rd Div. M.G.Coy.
    2. 168th Inf. Bde.   14. 56th Div. Signals.
    3. 169th Inf. Bde.   15. 56th Div. Train.
    4. VIIth Corps   16. Div. M.G.Officer.
    5. 14th Division.   17. Div. Gas Officer.
    6. 30th Division.   18. D.A.D.O.S.
    7. C.R.A.   19. 4th Aust. Div.Supply Col.
    8. C.R.E.   20. No. 2 Ammn. Sub Park.
    9. 1/5th Ches. Regt. 21. G.O.C.
   10. A.D.M.S.   22. A.D.C.
   11. "Q"   23. War Diary.
   12. A.P.M.   24. File.

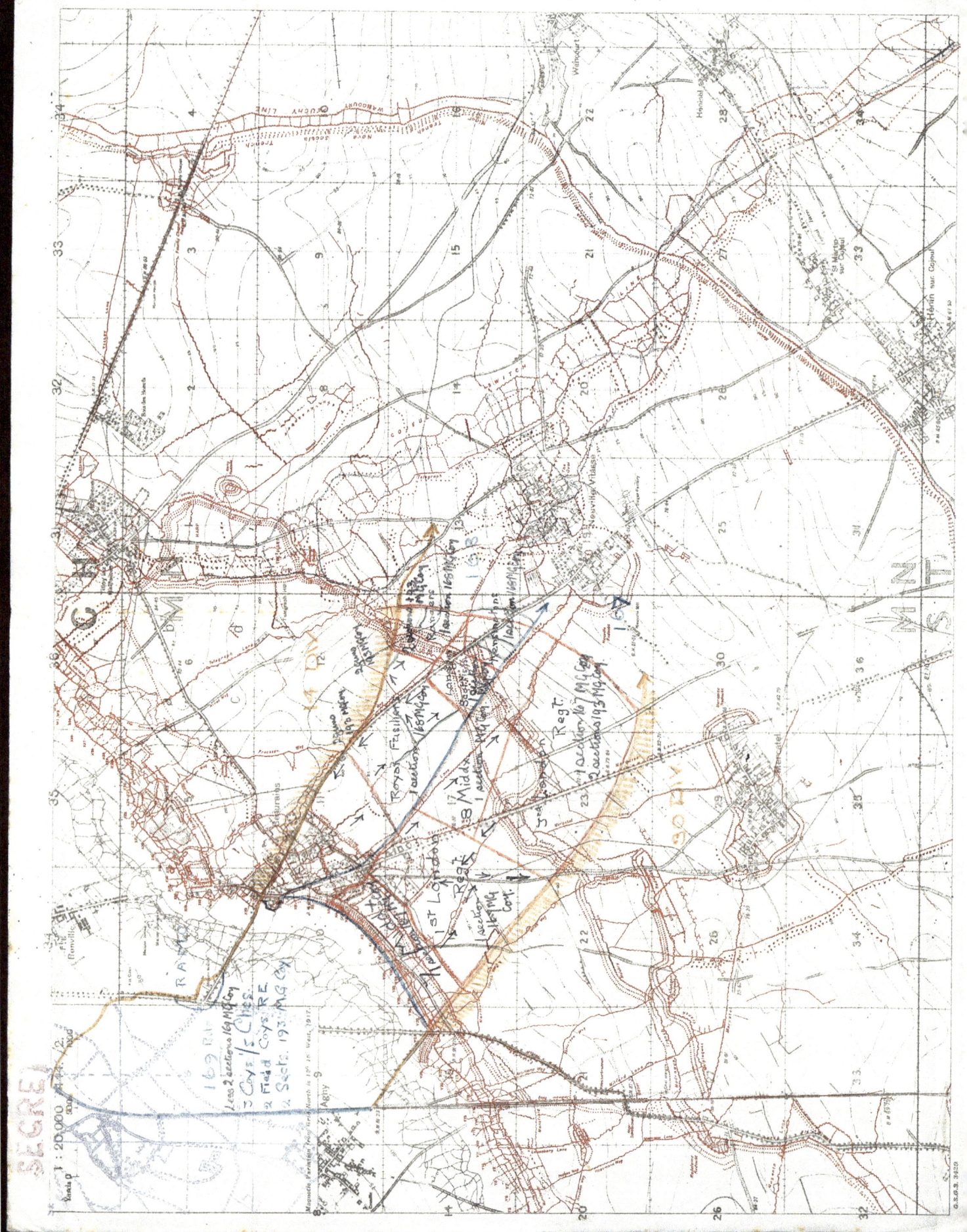

SECRET *War Diary*

56th Div. G.A.100.

167th Infantry Brigade.
168th Infantry Brigade.
169th Infantry Brigade.
C.R.A.
C.R.E.
1/5th Cheshire Regt.
A.D.M.S.
"Q"
A.P.M.
193rd Div.M.G.Coy.
56th Div. Signals.

56th Div. Train.
Div. M.G. Officer.
Div. Gas Officer.
D.A.D.O.S.
4th Aust.Div.Supply Column.
No.2 Ammn.Sub Park.
G.O.C.
A.D.C.
War Diary.
File.

From April 1st inclusive, all units will take steps to see that every Officer in the Division gets signal time every day, and sets his watch accordingly. Staffs and O.C's will verify that this has been done by personal checks as opportunities offer. This is essential so that there shall be no mistakes on Z day.

Head Qrs. 56th Divn.
30th March, 1917.

B. Pakenham
Lieut-Colonel,
General Staff.

War Diary

SECRET.   56th Divn. G.2/88.

56th DIVISION INSTRUCTIONS.

MAPS.

The following will be the Maps to be carried during forthcoming operations.

As far as the supply admits, each officer will be in possession of both maps. -

    1/20,000   SHEET 51 B. S.W.   Edition 4 A   (Trench Map)
    1/40,000   SHEET 51 B.   First Edition.

or SCARPE VALLEY

Head Qrs. 56th Divn.
31st March, 1917.

                                                Lieut-Colonel,
                                                General Staff.

Copies to -
167th Inf.Bde.	193rd Div.M.G.Coy.
168th Inf.Bde.	56th Div.Signals.
169th Inf.Bde.	56th Div. Train.
C.R.A.	D.A.D.O.S.
C.R.E.	4th Aust.Div.Supply Col.
1/5th Cheshire Regt.	No.2 Ammn.Sub Park.
A.D.M.S.	G.O.C.
"Q"	A.D.C.
A.P.M.	War Diary.
Div.M.G.Officer.	File.
Div. Gas Officer.	

SECRET.   56th Divn. No.G.A.103.

56th DIVISION INSTRUCTIONS.

EMPLOYMENT of R.E. & PIONEERS

1. R.E. & Pioneers will be attached to units for forthcoming operations as follows :-

    167th Inf. Bde.   H.Q. & 2 Sections 416th Field Coy.

    168th Inf. Bde. (H.Q. & 2 Sections 512th Field Coy.
                              (1 Coy. 1/5th Cheshire Regt.
                                                    (Pioneers)

2. The following R.E. & Pioneers will be under the orders of the C.R.E. -

    2 Sections 416th Field Coy. R.E.

    2 Sections 512th Field Coy. R.E.

    513th Field Coy. R.E.

    181st Tunnelling Coy. R.E.

    1/5th Cheshire Regt. (Pioneers) less one Company..

3. The R.E. & Pioneers attached to assaulting Brigades are allotted principally for the purpose of constructing strong points according to the success of the operations.

    Other tasks, such as those enumerated on page 31 of "Instructions for the Training of Divisions for Offensive Action" (S.S.135) will be carried out under the orders of the C.R.E.

4. The R.E. & Pioneers allotted to assaulting Brigades will come under the orders of their respective Brigade Commanders on Z - 1 day, but the Officers Commanding will report to the Brigade Commander for instructions when desired by the latter.

Head Qrs. 56th Divn.   Lieut-Colonel,
31st March, 1917.   General Staff.

Copies to -
    167th Infantry Bde.   56th Div. Signals.
    168th Infantry Bde.   56th Div. Train.
    169th Infantry Bde.   Div. M.G.Officer.
    C.R.A.   Div. Gas Officer
    C.R.E.   D.A.D.O.S.
    1/5th Cheshire Regt.   4th Aust. Div. Supply Column.
    A.D.M.S.   No. 2 Ammn. Sub Park.
    "Q"   G.O.C.
    A.P.M.   A.D.C.
    193rd Div.M.G.Coy.   War Diary.
                                            File.

War Diary

SECRET.

56th Divn. No.G.A.104.

56th DIVISION INSTRUCTIONS

ARRANGEMENTS FOR LIAISON WITH NEIGHBOURING UNITS.

1. **Between Div. H.Q. & Reserve Brigade.**

    (a). On "Z" day from Zero plus 2 hours, the G.O.C. 169th Infantry Brigade and the Divisional M.G.Officer will be at Advanced Divisional Headquarters which will be in dugouts under Railway Embankment at M.3.c.5.1.

    (b). Battalion Commanders of 169th Infantry Brigade, O.C. 169th T.M.Battery and Senior Officer i/c Reserve M.Gs. of 169th M.G. Coy. will be at 169th Brigade H.Q.

2. **Between Div. H.Q., C.R.A. and C.R.E.**

    The C.R.A. and C.R.E. will be at Advanced Divisional Headquarters.

    The C.R.E. will arrange for O.C. 513th Field Coy. R.E., O.C. Sections of 416th and 512th Field Coys. R.E. not allotted to Brigades, and for the O.C. Pioneer Battalion to be together at some convenient place where he can give them orders personally.

3. **Between Brigades and Flank Brigades.**

    Brigadier-Generals Commanding 167th and 168th Infantry Brigades will arrange for a Liaison Officer to be with the Brigade Headquarters on either Flank.

4. **Between Battalions and Flank Battalions.**

    Each Assaulting Battalion will have an Officer or reliable N.C.O. and 4 Runners with the Headquarters of the Battalion on either Flank.

5. **Between Infantry and Artillery.**

    A Senior Artillery Liaison Officer will be detailed to accompany the Headquarters of 167th and 168th Infantry Brigades throughout the operations.

    The C.R.A. will arrange for the attachment of a Liaison Officer to 169th Infantry Brigade, should the latter be committed to action.

    These Liaison Officers must be aware of all Artillery dispositions which may affect the Infantry Unit to which they are attached.

B. Pakenham
Lieut-Colonel,
General Staff.

Head Qrs. 56th Divn.
31st March, 1917.

Copies to -
- 167th Inf. Bde.
- 168th Inf. Bde.
- 169th Inf. Bde.
- C.R.A.
- C.R.E.
- 1/5th Cheshire Regt.
- 14th Division.
- 30th Division.
- VII Corps.
- A.D.M.S.
- "Q"
- A.P.M.
- 193rd Div.M.G.Coy.
- 56th Div. Signals.
- 56th Div. Train.
- Div. M.G.Officer.
- Div. Gas Officer.
- D.A.D.O.S.
- 4th Aust.Div.Supply Col.
- No. 2 Ammn.Sub Park.
- G.O.C.
- A.D.C.
- War Diary.
- File.

War Diary

SECRET   56th Divn.No.G.A.105.

56th DIVISION INSTRUCTIONS.

CONCENTRATION.

Ref attached Sketch Map.

1.   On Z - 3 & Z - 2 days at 10 a.m. the disposition of troops will be as under :-

        167th & 168th Infantry Brigades in the Line

        169th Infantry Brigade in Reserve

                                  (Brigade H.Qrs.
                    at MONCHIET. (3 Battalions
                                  (M.G.Coy.
                                  (T.M.Bty.

                    At BEAUMETZ (1 Battalion)

2.   On the night of Z - 2/Z - 1, the following moves will take place :-

        167th Infantry Brigade will move into Area "A"

        168th   "   "   "   "   " Area "B"

        169th   "   "   "   "   " Areas C & C1
                                  ACHICOURT & AGNY.

    Troops to be accommodated in these Areas are shewn on the Map.

    All moves will be completed by 6 a.m. on Z - 1 day.

3.   On Z - 1/Z night, Brigades will take over their assembly areas.

    A Map showing Assembly Areas was forwarded under Divisional Instructions "ASSEMBLY AREAS" Office No.G.A.96 of the 30th March.

    All moves will be complete by 3 a.m. Z day.

4.   Area C will be administered by Town Major, ACHICOURT.

        Area C1 "   "   "   "   "   " AGNY.

5.   ACKNOWLEDGE.

Head Qrs. 56th Divn.   Lieut-Colonel,
31st March, 1917.   General Staff.

Copies to:-

167th Inf.Bde.	A.P.M.	D.A.D.O.S.
168th Inf.Bde.	Town Major, AGNY.	4th Aust.Div.Sup.
169th Inf.Bde.	Town Major, ACHICOURT.	Column.
C.R.A.	193rd Div.M.G.Coy.	No.2 Amm.Sub Pk.
C.R.E.	56th Div.Signals.	G.O.C.
1/5th Ches. Regt.	56th Div. Train.	A.D.C.
A.D.M.S.	Div.M.G.Officer.	War Diary.
"Q"	Div. Gas Officer.	File.
VII Corps.	14th Division.	
	30th Division.	

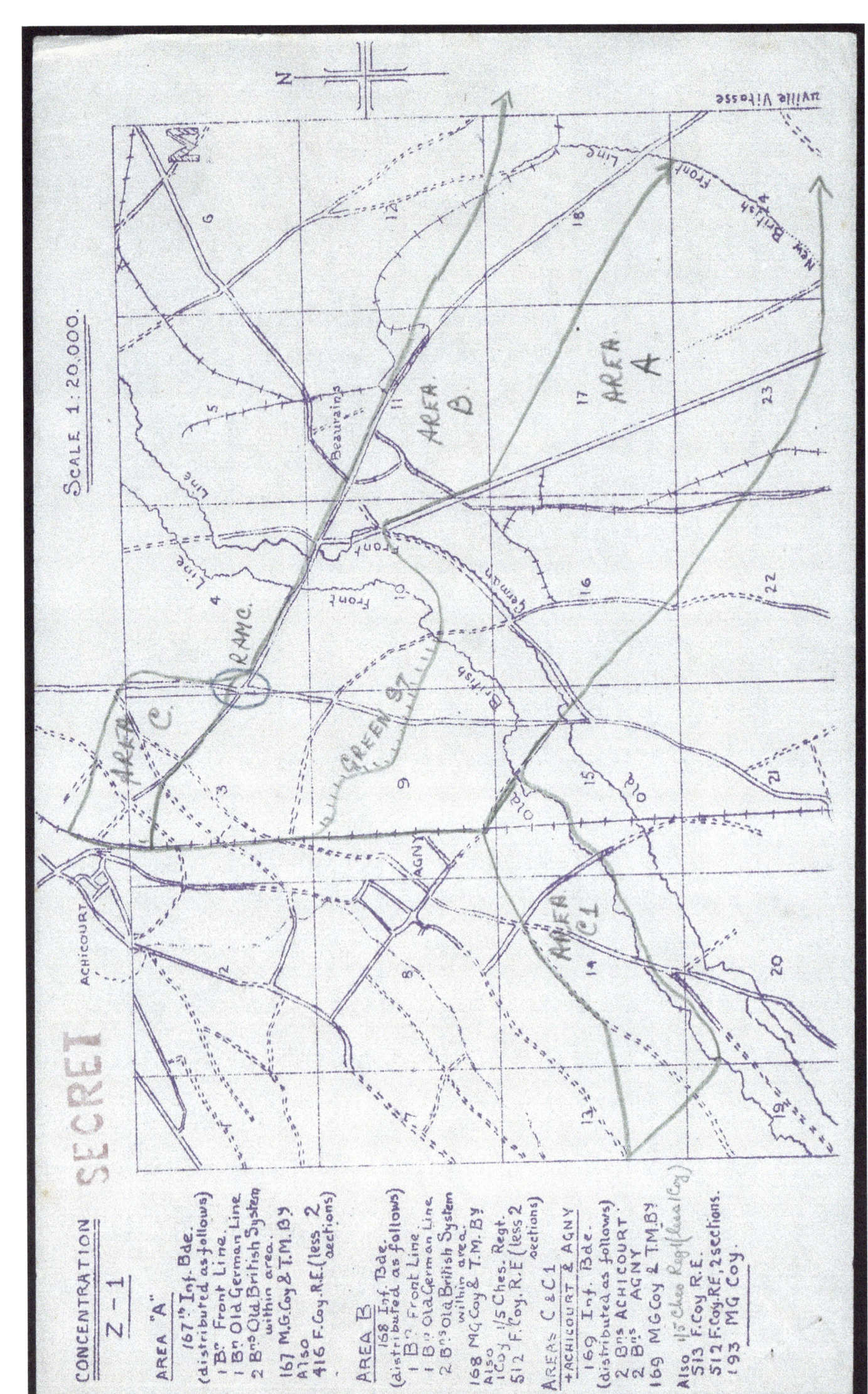

SECRET.   56th Divn. No.G.A.106

56th DIVISION INSTRUCTIONS.

OPERATIONS.

1. With reference to 56th Divisional Warning Order No. 77 of 22nd inst., Map A issued therewith is now cancelled, and the Map issued with 56th Division No. G.A.78 of 27th inst. will be substituted and marked "A".   The Dividing Line between 167th and 168th Infantry Brigades will remain unaltered up to and including the rear trench of the HINDENBURG LINE or COJEUL SWITCH.

2. The attack will be carried out by 167th Infantry Brigade on the right and by 168th Infantry Brigade on the left up to and inclusive of the rear trench of the HINDENBURG LINE or COJEUL SWITCH.

    From this line the attack on the BROWN Line will be carried out by the 167th Infantry Brigade.

3. The new Map "A" will be forwarded with the final Operation Order to those who have not already received 56th Division No. G.A.78 of 27th instant.

                                                B Pakenham
                                                Lieut-Colonel,
Head Qrs. 56th Divn.   General Staff.
31st March, 1917.

Copies to -
    167th Infantry Brigade.   A.P.M.
    168th Infantry Brigade.   193rd Div.M.G.Coy.
    169th Infantry Brigade.   56th Div.Signals.
    VII Corps.   "   "   Train.
     "   "   Artillery.   Div. M.G.Officer.
     "   "   Heavy Artillery.   Div. Gas Officer.
     "   "   M.G.Officer.   D.A.D.O.S.
    14th Division.   4th Aust. Div. Supply Column.
    30th Division.   No.2 Ammn.Sub Park.
    C.R.A.   G.O.C.
    C.R.E.   A.D.C.
    1/5th Cheshire Regt.   War Diary.
    A.D.M.S.   File.
    "Q"

Appendix D   War Diary

SECRET

OFFENSIVE OPERATIONS on VII CORPS FRONT.

56th Divisional Instructions No. 1.

Ref. LENS SHEET 11 - 1/100,000, and Trench Map.
NEUVILLE VITASSE - 1/10,000, and Sketch
Map attached.

General Plan. 1. (a). An attack is to be made by the Third Army with the object of capturing MERCATEL - Hill 90 (S.W. of WANCOURT) - the German 3rd line system from FEUCHY CHAPEL (N.3.b.) to FEUCHY and the high ground about MONCHY le PREUX.

(b). The VII Corps will be on the Right and will attack on the front AGNY - FICHEUX Road to the road running S.E. through G.36.c.

(c). The attack will be made by VII Corps with 3 Divisions -

30th Division on the Right.
56th   "   in the Centre.
14th   "   on the Left.

A fourth Division will be in Reserve.

Successive objectives. 2. The successive objectives of the VII Corps attack will be -

(a). The capture of the German 1st line system from the AGNY - FICHEUX Road to G.36.c. including the Village of BEAURAINS.

(b). The capture of the 2nd line system from about M.22.c.3.2. M.28.a.15.95. to N.1.d.1.0.

(c). The capture of the SCHLANGEN & ULRICH Redoubts & of NEUVILLE VITASSE.

(d). The capture of MERCATEL, the German 3rd line N.W. of HENINEL and also the hill (Hill 90) between that line and HENINEL.

The different phases of the attack are shown by the Black, Blue, Brown and Green lines on the accompanying Map "A"

/3.

Objectives of 56th Division.

3. The dividing lines between Divisions are shown on the accompanying Map "A"

Method of Attack.

4. (a). The attack will be carried out by the 56th Division with -

    167th Infantry Brigade on the Right.

    168th Infantry Brigade on the Left.

    169th Infantry Brigade in Reserve.

The dividing line between 167th & 168th Infantry Brigades is shown on attached Map "A".

(b). It is intended that the 167th and 168th Inf. Brigades should complete the capture of the first and second objectives as shown by the Black and Blue lines, and that the capture of the third and fourth objectives (Brown & Green Lines) should be carried out by 169th Infantry Brigade.

(c). It is estimated that the objectives will be reached as follows :-

Black Line - at Zero + 1 hour.
Halt one hour to allow of troops passing through for attack on Blue Line.

Leave Black Line - at Zero + 2 hours.

Reach Blue Line - at Zero + 2 hours 40 minutes.
Halt on Blue line for 4 hours to allow of troops passing through for attack on Brown Line.

Leave Blue Line - At Zero + 6 hours 40 minutes.

Reach Brown Line - At Zero + 8 hours 40 minutes.

Beyond Brown Line - No fixed programme - troops will push straight on, and the capture of the Green line should be completed by the 30th and 56th Divisions about 3 hours before darkness, each Division being supported in its advance by the artillery directly allotted to it.

(d). It is important that, while in occupation of the Blue line, the troops should reach points from which observation can be obtained over the whole of the ground up to the Brown Line.

/(e).

(e). After the capture of the Brown Line, (the beginning of open warfare), it must be realized that the maintenance of the forward movement depends on the determination and power of direction of sections, platoons, companies and battalions.

The habit of digging a trench and getting into it, or of waiting for scientifically arranged artillery barrages before advancing, must be discarded.

(f). A slow advance will give time for German reinforcements to arrive - the greater the rapidity of the advance, the more is resistance likely to lessen.

A few "sticky" Company Commanders may not only delay the whole operation, but by giving the enemy time to reinforce, will also cause unnecessary casualties.

(g). Whatever the positions gained at nightfall, strong outposts must be pushed well in front of our line during the hours of darkness, so as to prevent the Germans re-organizing and digging new lines. These outposts must be strongly entrenched.

Artillery. 5. (a). Exclusive of Heavy Artillery, there will be about 96 Field Guns or 4.5" Hows. covering the Divisional front.

(b). The number of Trench Mortars to be placed at the disposal of the Division will be (probably)

        9.45" Heavy T.M's.   16

        2"   Medium T.M's.   32

The destruction of the wire of the first line system will be chiefly carried out by these weapons.

(c). Wire cutting by Field Artillery & T.M's is to be commenced at once.

/(d).

(d). The Artillery preparation will be a bombardment of 48 hours duration; during this period the fire will be continuous and of equal cadence.

(e). Arrangements are to be made for 1/3 of the total number of guns and howitzers to be rested in turn; for the artillery personnel to be given 12 hours rest (officers & men) in 24 hours, and for the personnel of T.M. batteries to obtain sufficient rest.

(f). Artillery as well as Infantry must educate themselves for open warfare. When this phase is reached, Battery Commanders must be prepared to use their initiative, and to be able to make a rapid reconnaissance followed by rapid movement. Any fear of damage to horses and guns in endeavours to support the infantry at close range must not be considered and direct fire will become common.

Smoke. 6. A smoke screen will be formed on the right flank of 30th Division.

Gas. 7. Gas projectors ("L' Special Coy. R.E.) will be installed on the front of the 56th Division. Just before the commencement of the Artillery bombardment a flight of drums will be projected into BEAURAINS, if the conditions are favourable. They may also be used later.

Tanks. 8. Tanks will probably be available for the attack on the second line (Blue line) and possibly for "mopping up" the Black line.

Assembly Areas. 9. Assembly areas allotted to Infantry Brigades are shown in the accompanying Sketch "B".

Work on Line. 10. (a). A table showing work to be carried out in the line has already been issued to all concerned under 56th Division No. G.7/7 of 12th March, 1917.

As there has been insufficient time at present for thorough reconnaissance this must be considered as being issued only provisionally as a guide.

/(b).

(b). The General Officers Commanding 167th & 168th Infantry Brigades will make a reconnaissance of their respective areas and report to Div. H.Q. their requirements as regards -

    (a). Improving C.T's.

    (b). Provision of Assembly Trenches.

    (c). Provision of H.Qs. to supplement existing ones.

    (d). Improvement of signal communication.

    (e). Sites for Brigade and Battalion dumps - stores, rations and water.

    (f). Nature and number of bridges required.

    (g). Number of ladders required for assaulting troops.

    (h). Allotment of trenches for IN and OUT communication.

    (j). Aid Posts required.

    (k). Screening, etc.

Div. H.Q. will then instruct G.O.C., 169th Infantry Bde. regarding the above work in order of priority.

(c). All Brigadier-Generals Commanding will reconnoitre with a view to selecting tracks across country from the main ARRAS - DOULLENS Road to the RONVILLE - BOIRY - ST. RICTRUDE Road, so that troops may avoid main roads and the outskirts of ARRAS.

(d). The Brigadier-General Commanding 169th Brigade will cause a reconnaissance to be made of our own and the enemy wire along the Divisional front, and will render a report to Div. H.Q. as soon as possible, specifying the location and nature of existing gaps, which he will arrange to keep open.

T.M.Bombs. 11. The G.O.C., R.A. will calculate the amount of T.M. ammunition required for the operations, and arrange with Div. H.Q. for such carrying parties as may be required.

Machine Guns. 12. The Divisional M.G.Officer will make a reconnaissance with a view to covering the advance of the two leading Brigades by an indirect M.G.barrage on the slopes behind

/the

the German 1st line position, for which purpose the Div. M.G.Coy. will be available to co-operate with 167th & 168th M.G.Coys.

He will also consider the question of the further employment of machine guns to cover the advance beyond the Black Line and submit proposals to Div. H.Q.; in this advance direct overhead barrage fire can probably be brought to bear on the German positions beyond each successive objective and machine guns can be pushed forward for the close support of the infantry under cover of other machine guns in rear.

Any opportunities for training must be utilized to practice this open warfare, particular attention being directed to the teams not presenting a marked target, especially when they come under direct hostile observation.

B Pakenham

Head Qrs. 56th Divn.
13th March, 1917.

Lieut-Colonel,
General Staff.

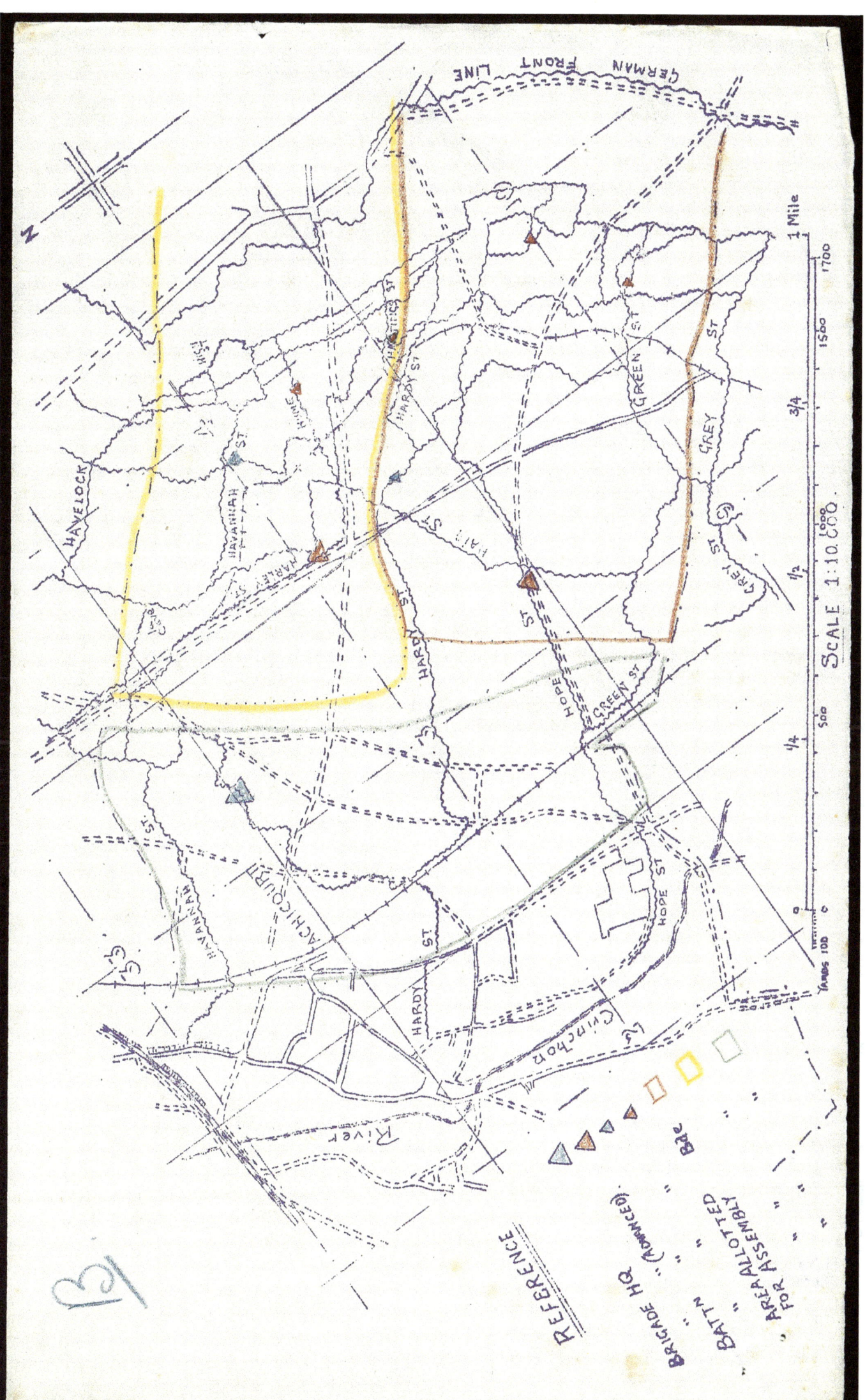

War Diary

Appendix E

XI Corps RHS.1194/8.   56th Divn.G.434.

The G.O.C., 56th Division.

On the departure of your Division, I am anxious to place on record my appreciation of the excellent work done by the Commanders, Staff and all ranks throughout the Division during the time it has been in the XI Corps.

In its higher leading and Staff work the Division is conspicuous for sound tactical judgment and forethought, and for its cheeriness and good fellowship in all its dealings, both with those above and below.

In the Unit, Brigade and Divisional Headquarters I have always found that the basis of work is to help everyone else and not to make difficulties. A large number of Regimental Officers have been efficiently trained in staff work and have proved their value when they have been given definite appointments.

The fighting spirit of all ranks is excellent, and this has been shown with the greatest success by the prosecution of raids into the enemy's lines, and by the operations carried out in bitter weather during January, when the front system of the German trenches was held by the Division in a series of posts, and all attacks repelled with success until orders were received to withdraw.

The scouting, sniping, observation, wiring and work on the defences by the Infantry; the accurate and immediate application of fire whenever required, and the construction of spare Observation Posts and Battery positions by the Artillery; the skilful work of the Royal Engineer Companies in the line, and the administration of the back area as regards supplies of food and ammunition and the care of the sick and wounded leave nothing to be desired. I also wish to thank the Chaplains of all denominations in the Division for their devoted work to officers and men both in and out of the trenches.

The football competitions got up by the Divisional Commander and the excellent entertainments provided by the "Bow Bell" troupe have greatly assisted all of us to keep cheery and lively during the winter months.

I have no hesitation in saying that this Division is one of the best that has been in my Corps, and there have been over twenty in it since it was first formed. I am convinced that wherever the Division goes, and whatever it is called upon to do, the officers non-commissioned officers and men will always distinguish themselves.

I wish the Division an early victory to add to others it has already gained, and I part with it with the deepest regret which is shared by all my staff.

7th March, 1917.   (Sgd.) R.HAKING, Lieut-General,
                                              Commanding XI Corps.

For information and communication to all concerned.

Head Qrs. 56th Divn.
8th March, 1917.   Lieut-Colonel,
                                                  General Staff.

"A" Form.				Army Form C.2121
MESSAGES AND SIGNALS.				(in pads of 100). No. of Message......
Prefix......Code......m.	Words	Charge	*This message is on a/c of:*	Recd. at......m.
Office of Origin and Service Instructions.	Sent			Date......
By DR	At......m.		Service.	From......
	To			
	By		(Signature of "Franking Officer.")	By......
TO { All Batns PIP			2Lds	Ja

Sender's Number.	Day of Month.	In reply to Number.	
SC ~~788~~ 860	31/3		AAA

Reference AQS/216 of 30 inst AAA Para 5 AAA Trench stellers have been drawn and will be distributed by Bde T.O. as follows: ATTEN DICK PIP 7 each BAT SHOU 8 each BdeHQ + Signals 3 AAA Advt all Battalions PIP

From RE
Place
Time 6 15 pm

The above may be forwarded as now corrected. (Z)

Censor. Signature of......
* This line should be erased
750,000. W 2186—M509 H. W. & V., Ld. 6/16.

SECRET.

INSTRUCTIONS REGARDING RATIONS DURING THE FORTHCOMING OPERATIONS.

1. Three days iron rations (additional to the normal iron ration always carried on the man) will be issued as soon as possible, for consumption on Z+1, Z+2, and Z+3, days, to the whole Division.

2. No other rations will be issued for consumption on the above days.

3. The object in issuing these rations is to keep transport clear of roads during the above period.

4. These rations will be dumped in accordance with attached Table "A".

5. (a) The whole of the rations to be dumped at each Brigade dump and at the gun positions will in the first instance be dumped at a spot in the vicinity of AGNY CHATEAU M.2.c.7.0., sheet 51 B, under arrangements to be made by O.C. Divisional Train.

(b) Infantry Brigades will draw 3 days iron rations for all ranks, other than those left in the transport lines, and Divisional Artillery will draw one day's iron rations for all ranks in gun positions from the above dump through their Formation Supply Officer.
Infantry Brigades will include in this ration strength One Field Company R.E.

(c) The rations mentioned in para.(b) will be dumped under arrangements to be made by 167th and 168th Infantry Brigades, and C.R.A.
In the case of 169th Infantry Brigade these rations will be dumped under arrangements to be made by O.C. Divisional Train, near AGNY – CHATEAU.

(d) In forming Brigade Dumps, the following procedure will be followed. The Formation concerned is responsible for selecting and preparing the site of the dump, and for dumping the rations. Once the rations are dumped they will be taken over by the Formation Supply Officer concerned, who will be responsible for their custody and for their daily issue to Units.
In selecting sites for dumps it must be borne in mind that, should a forward movement take place, all rations remaining at the dumps will have to be brought on at once by either First Line Transport or by the Divisional Train, as they will be, until Z+4 day, the only rations available for consumption – sites of dumps therefore should if possible be near roads. It is suggested that all arrangements for forming these dumps by Formations should be carried out in conjunction with their Formation Supply Officer.

6. Iron rations and oats to be dumped with Units or at First Line Transport Lines in accordance with attached Table "A", will be delivered at those places in bulk by O.C. Divl. Train by Z day, the Units concerned making the detail issues each day.

7. Iron rations and Oat Rations for "Other Divisional Troops" will be issued daily by Divisional Train.

8. The three days iron rations for 1/5th Cheshire Regt. and for 193 Machine Gun Company will be dumped by Divl. Train, in accordance with Table "A", and will be taken on charge by Supply Officer 169th Infantry Brigade, on whom these Units will indent for their rations during this period.

9. Should it be necessary to move these rations, they will as far as possible be carried on First Line Transport. Application will at once be made to affiliated Train Companies for transport for rations which cannot be so carried.

10. It must be clearly understood that these rations are in no way a reserve, but are for normal consumption during the period in question.

F. Phenoph. Major,
D/A.Q.M.G., 56th Divisi

26.3.17.

"A"

S E C R E T.

SITUATION OF DUMPED RATIONS ON Z DAY.

	With Unit.	In Div. Advanced Dump. AGNY CHATEAU.	In Brigade Dump.	At Gun positions.	At First Line Transport Lines.	With Divl. Train.
167 Brigade } One Field Coy. RE. }	-	Nil.	3 days iron rations.	-	3 days iron rations for personnel. 3 days oat rations.	-
168 Brigade } One Field Coy. RE. }	-	Nil.	3 days iron rations.	-	3 days iron rations for personnel. 3 days oat rations.	-
169 Brigade } One Field Coy. RE. }	-	3 days iron rations.	Nil.	-	3 days iron rations for personnel. 3 days oat rations.	-
Div. Arty. less D.A.C.	-	Nil.	Nil.	1 days iron rations for gunners	3 days iron rations for drivers. 2 days iron rations for gunners. 3 days oat rations.	-
D.A.C.	3 days iron rations. 3 days oat rations.	(rations. 3 days iron	-	-	(3 days iron rations (for personnel. (3 days oat rations.	-
5th Cheshire Rgt.	-	-do-	-	-	-do-	-
193 Machine Gun Coy	-	-	-	-	-do-	-
Each Field Ambce.	3 days iron rations.	-	-	-	-	-
Other Div. Troops. }	-	-	-	-	(3 days iron rations. (3 days oat rations.	-
Attached Units.	3 days iron rations.	-	-	-	3 days oat rations.	-

466

SECRET.

56th Divn.
AQS/216.

ADMINISTRATIVE INSTRUCTIONS (1) FOR OFFENSIVE OPERATIONS.

1. RATIONS.
2. REINFORCEMENTS. } = Instructions have already been issued on these subjects.
3. SALVAGE.

4. **AMMUNITION & WATER.**

   (1)　The 167th and 168th Infantry Brigades will each form a Brigade Dump containing the ammunition and water shown on the attached Table "A".

   (2)　These Brigade Dumps will be stocked from the Divisional Advanced Dump situated at AGNY CHATEAU M.2.c.7.0., Sheet 51 B.

   (3)　All Grenades issued from the Divisional Dump will, as far as possible, be detonated before issue.

   (4)　Table "A" shows the amount of Ammunition and Water at each Dump.

5. **Q. M. STORES and FIRST LINE TRANSPORT.**

   (1)　The First Line Transport and Quartermaster's stores of Units will be established as follows :-

Units.	Transport.		Q. M. Stores.
	Site.	Trench Shelters.	
167th Infantry Bde.	M.2.c.	40	AGNY.
168th "	G.32.a.	40	ACHICOURT.
169th "	G.32.a.	40	ACHICOURT.
5th Cheshire Regt.	G.32.a.	12	ARRAS.
193rd Machine Gun Cy.	G.32.a.	8	ACHICOURT.
416th (Edin) Fld. Cy.	G.32.a.	8	ACHICOURT.
512th (London) "	M.2.c.	–	AGNY.
513th (") "	G.32.a.	8	ACHICOURT.

   (2)　The exact site of Transport Lines will be pointed out by Town Majors concerned.
   　　Trench Shelters to the number shown on the above Table will be issued to Brigade Transport Officers and to the Transport Officers of the Pioneer Battalion, Machine Gun Company and Field Companies by the Town Major of ACHICOURT. These shelters will be returned to the Town Major in the event of a further move, and under no circumstances will they be removed from the village area.

   (3)　Q.M. Stores will be accommodated in buildings on application to Town Majors concerned.

P.T.O.

6. **BLANKETS, LEATHER JERKINS, PACKS and SURPLUS STORES.**

   (1) The second blanket will be handed in by Units at the D.A.D.O.S. Stores on dates as follows :-

Units.	Dates.	Transport.
167th Infantry Brigade.	March 30th.)	1st Line Transport and Baggage wagons.
168th "	" ")	"
169th "	April 4th	"
5th Cheshire Regt.	" 2nd	"
193rd Machine Gun Coy.	" 2nd.	"
Batteries R.F.A.)	" 3rd	"
M. and H.T.M. Batteries.)		
Field Companies, R.E.	" 2nd	"

   Other Units will retain the second blanket for the present.

   (2) Any further surplus baggage or stores which can be disposed of to the Divisional Dump at FREVENT will be sent to the Town Major BEAUMETZ who will arrange for a store and guard. Divisional arrangements will be made to transport this to FREVENT.

   (3) The first blanket of Infantry Brigades, Pioneer Battalion and Divl. M. Gun Coy. will be stored at Quartermaster's Stores, where they will be retained pending developments.

   (4) Infantry Brigade Commanders will make such arrangements as they consider necessary for the storage of packs, but under no circumstances will these be stacked in either ACHICOURT or AGNY in buildings which can be used as billets for Troops.

   (5) Leather jerkins may be either retained with Units or stored at Q.M.Stores at the discretion of Infantry Brigade Commanders.

7. **SURPLUS PERSONNEL.**

   The personnel of Units referred to in "Instructions for the Training of Divisions for Offensive Action", (SS135) Section XXX, as amended, will be billeted at or near the Quartermaster's Stores of their Units under close billeting arrangements, where accommodation will be reserved by Town Majors for the approximate number of 50 Officers and 450 men per Infantry Brigade.

8. **RUM, SOUP, SANDWICHES.**

   (1) It is hoped to be able to issue 2 Oxo Cubes or pea Soup to Infantry Brigades, Pioneer Bn., Artillery Batteries and Field Companies, on Z - 1 Day.

   (2) Rum will be issued on Z - 1 Day.

   (3) It is suggested that a portion of the bacon ration be retained and made into cold bacon sandwiches for consumption on Z Day under Unit arrangements.

9. **TELESCOPES and TELESCOPIC RIFLES.**

   Telescopes and Telescopic Rifles will not be taken into action but will be carefully stored in their cases at Quartermaster's Stores.
   Care is to be taken that Telescopic Rifles are sent by hand and not taken in wagons.

10. VETERINARY ARRANGEMENTS.

An Advanced Veterinary Collecting Station will be established under the arrangements of the A.D.V.S. for the reception of sick and wounded horses in the vicinity of AGNY CHATEAU.

The Mobile Veterinary Section will remain at BEAUMETZ.

11. POSTAL ARRANGEMENTS.

Divisional and Brigade Field post Offices will be attached to affiliated Companies of the Divisional Train from Z - 1 day after the delivery of the mails.

12. PRISONERS.

All prisoners will be sent to a Collecting post which will be established and marked at M.4.d.1.1. and where they will be taken over by the A.P.M.

Prisoners will subsequently be escorted under arrangements to be made by the A.P.M. to the Divisional Cage in the Railway Cutting near ACHICOURT station prior to removal to the Corps Cage which has been prepared at BERNEVILLE.

13. STRAGGLERS.

The 167th and 168th Infantry Brigades will establish such Straggler posts as may be necessary.

The A.P.M. will arrange to post Military police at Advanced Dressing Stations, and Walking Wounded Collecting posts to deal with any men handed over to them by the Medical Officers in charge.

Advanced Dressing Stations and Walking Wounded Collecting post will be visited at frequent intervals by an Officer and escort to be detailed by each Brigade from those not going into action. These Officers will take over any Stragglers and will arrange for them to be sent to rejoin their Units on the first opportunity.

14. LOOTING.

All ranks are to be warned that the most extreme disciplinary action will be taken in the case of any soldier detected looting, or found in possession of, or to have disposed of any article from the dead

15. CHAPLAINS.

Senior Chaplains will arrange in co-operation with each other to leave certain Chaplains with Infantry Brigades, and to detail the remainder to assist at Advanced Dressing Stations, Walking Wounded Collecting posts and the Main Dressing Station.

The Senior Chaplain C of E. will establish himself at the Walking Wounded Collecting post at AGNY.

The Senior Chaplain Non C of E. will establish himself at the Advanced Dressing Station at ACHICOURT.

30.3.17.

Lieut. Colonel,
A.A.& Q.M.G., 56th Division

CONTENTS OF AMMUNITION & WATER DUMPS.

	To be dumped by 167th Inf.Bde.	To be dumped by 168th Inf.Bde.	Advanced Div. Dump. AGNY CHATEAU.	Corps Reserve Dump. Rue Joffre, ACHICOURT.
S.A.A.	250 boxes.	250 boxes.	500 Boxes	1500 boxes.
No. 5 Grenades.	10,000 (all to be detonated).	10,000 (all to be detonated).	20,000 (10,000 of which to be detonated).	60,000.
Rifle "	2,000 (all to be detonated).	2,000 (all to be detonated).	3,000 (2000 to be detonated).	40,000
3" Stokes T.M.	4,000	4,000	6,000	
Very pistol. 1" Ordinary. 1½" " 1" Green. 1½" Green.	1,000 1,000 150 500	1,000 1,000 150 500	3,000 2,000 200 1,000	5,000 8,000 500 2,000
Rockets.	100 S.O.S.	100 S.O.S.	100 of each colour.	
Portfires.	100	100	200	
Aeroplane Flares.	2,000	2,000	8,000	10,000
Water.	600 Petrol tins.	600 petrol tins.	500 petrol tins.	

TABLE "A".

"A"

S E C R E T.

SITUATION OF DUMPED RATIONS ON Z DAY.

	With Unit.	In Div. Advanced Dump. AGNY CHATEAU.	In Brigade Dump.	At Gun positions.	At First Line Transport Lines.	With Divl. Train.
167 Brigade One Field Coy. RE.	-	Nil.	3 days iron rations.	-	3 days iron rations for personnel. 3 days oat rations.	-
188 Brigade One Field Coy. RE.	-	Nil.	3 days iron rations.	-	3 days iron rations for personnel. 3 days oat rations.	-
169 Brigade One Field Coy. RE.	-	3 days iron rations.	Nil.	-	3 days iron rations for personnel. 3 days oat rations.	-
Div. Arty. less D.A.C.	-	Nil.	Nil.	1 days iron rations for gunners	3 days iron rations for drivers. 2 days iron rations for gunners. 3 days oat rations.	-
D.A.C.	3 days iron rations. 3 days oat rations.	-	-	-	-	-
5th Cheshire Rgt.	-	3 days iron rations.	-	-	{3 days iron rations for personnel.} {3 days oat rations.}	-
193 Machine Gun Coy.	-	-do-	-	-	-do-	-
Each Field Ambce.	3 days iron rations.	-	-	-	-do-	-
Other Div. Troops.	-	-	-	-	{3 days iron rations} {3 days oat rations.}	-
Attached Units.	3 days iron rations.	-	-	-	3 days oat rations.	-

First Series

W 74—664 250,000 3/15 L.S. & Co.   Army Form W. 3091.

Cover for Documents.

Secret

Nature of Enclosures.

File "D"

Offensive Operations on VII Corps front

Operation Orders from neighbouring Divisions

1917 MAR

Notes, or Letters written.

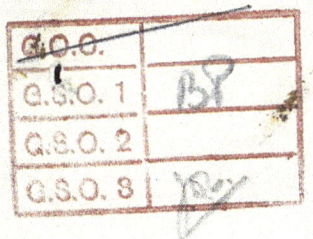

SECRET.

Copy No.... 1

30th DIVISION OPERATION ORDER NO. 59.

18th March, 1917.

Reference Trench Map and attached Map.

1. 30th Division Operation Orders 57 and 58 are cancelled.

2. The enemy's withdrawal to main defensive line COJEUL SWITCH EASTERN PORTION of NEUVILLE VITASSE inclusive – W. end of HARP TILLOY, will probably be carried out rapidly. 58th Division are in possession of BLAIREVILLE and FICHEUX. 56th Division are in BEAURAINS, 89th Infantry Brigade are in possession of MARLBOROUGH Trench.

3. The 89th Infantry Brigade will keep close touch with the enemy on their front and occupy the ground as he vacates it.
The Green Lines on attached map show the boundaries between Divisions in this forward move.
The Black Line shows the position to be secured first. From that line 89th Inf: Bde: will feel its way forward to the Blue Line. Eventually it may be possible for it to establish itself on the Blue dotted line.
The forward movement following the course of the enemy's withdrawal will probably develope from the right and be taken up by Divisions in succession from the right. The advance will be carried out cautiously and Brigades will avoid becoming involved in a serious engagement at present.

4. The 89th Inf: Bde: will concentrate in AGNY and forward area as opportunity arises. Brigade H.Q. will move to AGNY.

5. 1 Battalion 21st Inf: Bde: will move to ARRAS as soon as it is dark, the remainder 21st Inf: Bde: will be ready to move at 1 hour's notice to support 89th Inf: Bde:

6. 1 Battalion 90th Infantry Brigade will move to BEAUMETZ to-day as already arranged. Remainder 90th Inf: Bde: will be ready to move at 1 hour's notice to replace 21st Inf: Bde: in BEAUMETZ Area.

7. 30th Divl: Artillery will move forward by echelons to forward positions in the CRINCHON VALLEY.

8. 200th and 202nd Field Coy: R.E. will be at the disposal of 89th Inf: Bde:

9. 201st Field Coy: R.E. and Pioneer Battalion will be at the disposal of C.R.E.

10. 89th Inf: Bde: will report progress frequently, completion of all moves to be reported to this Office.

11. ACKNOWLEDGE.

Major,
General Staff.

Issued to Signals........2.30 p.m.

P.T.O.

Copy No.1.	56th Division.
2.	58th Division.
3.	30th Divl: Artillery.
4.	30th Divl: Engineers.
5.	21st Infantry Brigade.
6.	89th Infantry Brigade.
7.	90th Infantry Brigade.
8	11th South Lancs Regt:
9.	Divl: Train.
10.	A.D.M.S.
11.	Signal Coy.
12.	Divl: School
13.	Divl: Depot.
14.	A.A.& Q.M.G.
15.	G. File.
16.)	War Diary.
17.)	

SECRET

Copy No. 23

14th DIVISION OPERATION ORDER No. 108.

18th March, 1917.

Reference 1/10,000 Trench Map.

1. (i). The enemy has begun his withdrawal opposite the Corps on our right all of whose leading troops have now crossed into the German trenches.

   (ii). The right of the 30th Division has begun to feel forward and is reported to have occupied parts of MARLBOROUGH Trench.

   (iii). The 56th Division have entered old German front line south west of BEAURAINS and are moving northwards towards BEAURAINS.

   (iv). It is probable that the enemy will now withdraw quickly to his main defensive line - THE HARP, NICE TRENCH, COJEUL SWITCH, eastern half of NEUVILLE Village. (VITASSE)

2. (i). The 43rd and 42nd Infantry Brigades will keep close touch with the enemy on their front and occupy the ground as he vacates it. Brigades will avoid becoming involved in a serious engagement at present.

   (ii). The map attached to starred copies of these orders shows -

   (a) boundaries between Divisions in green.
   (b) boundaries between Brigades in brown.
   (c) the first objective to be aimed at in black.
   (d) further positions to be secured as opportunities present in blue.

   (iii). The forward movement will probably develop from the right and be taken up by Brigades in succession from the right.

   (iv). The 42nd Infantry Brigade will be responsible for forming the defensive flank. As a preliminary this flank should first be formed approximately on the prolongation of HALIFAX STREET and push forward as required.

3. The 14th Divisional Artillery has been placed at the disposal of the Division.

   C.R.A. will prepare to move forward the two rearmost batteries to positions in G 33 b. and d.

4. (i). The 7th Rif. Bde. will concentrate at DAINVILLE and be ready to move forward at short notice.

   (ii). The Field Companies and Pioneer Battalion less the two companies now attached to Infantry Brigades will assemble at their billets in ARRAS, collect tools and be ready to move out to work as may be ordered.

   (iii). The remainder of the 41st Inf. Bde. and the battalions of the 42nd and 43rd Inf. Bdes. now at GRAND RULLECOURT and SOMBRIN will stand by ready to move at 2 hours notice.

5. Artillery and Inf. Bdes. in line will make frequent reports of the situation.

Issued at 1.45 p.m.

Lieut Colonel
General Staff.

Distribution overleaf.

Copies to -

No. 1.* 14th Div. Artillery.
　2.* C.R.E.
　3.* 41st Infantry Bde.
　4.* 42nd Infantry Bde.
　5.* 43rd Infantry Bde.
　6.)
　7.) A.A. & Q.M.G.
　8.　14th Signal Coy.
　9.　11th King's Liverpool Regt.
　10.　14th Div. Train.
　11.　S.S.O.
　12.　14th Div. Supply Col.
　13.　A.D.M.S.
　14.　A.D.V.S.
　15.　D.A.D.O.S.
　16.　A.P.M.
　17.　14th Div. Depot Battalion.
　18.　14th Div. Gas Officer.
　19.　Camp Commandant.
　20.　VII Corps.
　21.　VII Corps H.A.
　22.　3rd Division.
　23.　56th Division.
　24.　War Diary.
　25.　File.

First Series

W 74—664 250,000 3/15 L.S. & Co.   Army Form W. 3091.

Cover for Documents.

Secret

Nature of Enclosures.

File B.2.

Offensive Operations on VII Corps front

Correspondence from Brigades &c

1917 MHK

Base 19/3/17

Notes, or Letters written.

File B2

Subject:- REPORTS ON WIRE ENTANGLEMENTS. B.M.912.

> GENERAL STAFF,
> 56th DIVISION.
> No. GA 35
> G.O.C.
> G.S.O. 1
> G.S.O. 2
> G.S.O. 3

Headquarters,
   56th Division.

Forwarded herewith reports on our own and the enemy wire along the Divisional front, in accordance with 56th Divisional instructions No.1, para. 10, sub-para (d) of 13th March, 1917.

18th March, 1917.

E. S. Coke. Brig. Genl.
Commdg. 169th Inf. Bde.

REPORT ON GERMAN WIRE ENTANGLEMENTS
H.1 SECTOR.

The enemy wire entanglements on this front seem fairly strong with few or no weak places. No gaps have been discovered.

	RIGHT.	OPPOSITE OUR CENTRE.	LEFT.
(a) Number of rows	1	2	2
(b) Type of entanglement.	Thick mass of double, crossed wire reinforced with wire balls	i. Knife rests wired together. ii. Thick wire entg'mt on 4 ft. stakes Width, 15 yds.	i. Trip wire ii. Wire entanglement on 4 ft. stakes reinforced with knife rests.
(c) Nature of wire used.	Thick Barbed.	Barbed.	Barbed.
(d) Trip wires.	Trip wire close to entg'mt.	NIL.	Trip wire.
(e) Distance of wire from enemy parapet.	30 - 40 yds.	40 yds.	30 - 40 yds.
(f) Average width and height.	18 yds. 3 ft. 6 ins.	20 yds. 4 ft.	15 yds. 3 - 5 ft.
(g) Existence of gaps.	NIL.	NIL.	NIL.

The reconnaissance of the enemy wire undertaken on two successive nights by our patrols was rendered difficult owing to the alertness of the enemy, and their bringing machine gun and rifle fire into play with the aid of constant VERY Lights. 77 mm. Field Guns were also fired into NO MAN'S LAND at one of our patrols.

17.3.17.

REPORT ON BRITISH WIRE ENTANGLEMENTS
H.1 SECTOR.

1. The wire entanglements along the whole Battalion front vary in strength, but on the whole present a moderate obstacle. It consists either of

    (a) Two belts of regulation wire entanglement with stakes, each belt about 8 to 10 yds. wide, and 10 to 15 yds interval.

or   (b) One belt as in (a), and a line of knife rests wired together.

RIGHT COMPANY.
- H.23.) Wire is very good and in fairly
- H.24.) strong condition.
- H.25.   Good in places. Weak spots opposite L.G. Post in Bay H.25. 12 and between Bay H.25 15 to H.25 Sap.
- H.26 to HOPE ST. Rt.   There are a number of stakes here, but very little wire, and there are many gaps.

CENTRE COMPANY.
- H.26 from HOPE ST. Rt.   Wire is fairly good consisting of (a).
- H.27.   The wire is not so good though there are a number of stakes in the ground
- H.28.   The wire is weak and much cut about.

LEFT COMPANY.
- H.29.) There is a fair obstacle of knife
- H.30.) rests wired together in places double.
- H.31.   Indifferent. The entanglement is wider here than usual, but has no system, and has been somewhat destroyed by shell fire.
- H.32.) Bad. Consists of apron and trip wire
- H.33.) with other entanglements which have also been damaged.

N.B.   The wire on this front has probably been fairly strong, but weak places caused by shell fire and other causes have not been repaired.

17.3.17.

SECRET

168th. Inf. Bde. No. 0/2.

Headquarters,

56th. Division.

168th. Infantry Brigade

Reconnaissance of the Area in Sector "H", allotted to this Brigade in accordance with 56th. Division Instructions No. 1 dated 13:3:17 - para. 10 (b).

Existing C.Ts. HAVANNAH. W. of the BUCQUOY ROAD not used, condition bad, E. of this road to the front line at present very muddy and difficult for traffic.

HUME. From BUCQUOY ROAD to front line condition poor, very muddy and difficult for traffic.

HASTINGS. A branch of HARDY and as such only useful between the Support Line and front line. The short run up trenches between Support and front line are generally in poor condition.

Proposed C.T. as suggested in tracing forwarded with your No. G.7/7 dated 12th. March 1917, would be of value for the Right Battalions - other proposals for improving C.Ts are shewn on Map "D".
Generally much work is required on all C.Ts, to make them easily passable - and passing places in all main C.Ts will be required.

2. ASSEMBLY TRENCHES. (See map "A" attached). It is roughly calculated from trenches shewn on only maps at present available that in each Battalion Area there exists at present the amount of trench accommodation available for assembly purposes as follows:-

Left Front Battalion.		
Front Trench	300 - 450	yards.
Control "	250 - 300	yards.
Close Support "	250 - 350	yards.
Support "	300 - 350	yards.
	1100 - 1400	yards

Right Front Battalion.		
Front "	400 - 450	yards
Control"	400	yards
Close Support "	300 - 500	yards
Support "	300	yards
	1400 - 1600	yards

RESERVE
~~Left Support~~ Battalion.

Reserve Line	350	yards
HARLEY STREET	350	yards
	700	yards

"BLUE LINE"
~~Right Support~~ Battalion.   Reserve Line 200 yards
                                HARLEY STREET 200 yards
                                ─────
                                          400 yards
                                          =====

Allowing 1½ yards a man for Battalions at an average strength of 750 (less Battalion H.Q.) there would appear to be sufficient existing accommodation for the forward Battalions, but not, in the case of the Right Battalion far enough forward, while as regards the Support Battalions more assembly trenches will need to be dug. No account has as yet been taken of the accommodation required for/Pioneer and R.E. Coy. which may be allotted.
      any
(It is hoped to send C.Os forward very shortly to carry out the necessary detailed reconnaissance of their areas on this subject).

3. ADVANCED BRIGADE AND BATTALION BATTLE H.Q.   These have been chosen and are shewn on Map "A". Included with them are M.G. Coy. and L.T.M. Battery H.Q. The dug-outs are generally good mined dug-outs with at least 2 entrances. The following work is still required.

Advanced Brigade H.Q.   Construction of dug-outs and connecting tunnels. At present there are only three shafts ending in nothing. Sufficient accommodation for Group R.A. must also be remembered, this must be actually adjoining.

Right Support Battalion.   Requires enlarging and deepening, at present accommodation inadequate.

Left Support Battalion.   Not yet started, a dugout with a minimum of 2 entrances 20 feet below ground, with accommodation for Battalion H.Q. is required.

Remainder are satisfactory, having in view the possible short time available and urgency of other work.

4. SIGNAL COMMUNICATIONS.   No information was available, but I saw cable being buried in~~we~~ a trench close to Advanced Brigade H.Q. A system of buried and trenched cables as shewn on Map "B" is required if possible, to ensure communication with all units of the Brigade. Communications forward of Battalion Headquarters will have to be by lines laid in C.Ts, rabbit netting over the open, runners etc.

5. SITES FOR BRIGADE AND BATTALION DUMPS ETC.

The ACHICOURT - BEAURAINS ROAD as far as the Cross roads in M.4.c is at present used for rations, R.E. Stores, etc. but this road would probably be common to both Brigades, as the right Brigade has no road available. This will increase the difficulties of forming the necessary dumps. The ARRAS - BUCQUOY ROAD will probably not be available for this Brigade.
The sites at present selected (which are subject to slight alteration) are shewn on Map "C". The principle aimed at is to form advanced dumps in the front or control trench and 3 in the support line on a larger scale near the C.Ts, with one or two Brigade Dumps, near the IN C.Ts.

6. **NATURE AND NUMBER OF BRIDGES REQUIRED.** Information not yet
available. Will be communicated later.

7. **NUMBER OF LADDERS REQUIRED FOR ASSAULTING TROOPS.** Approximately
450, allowing 1 per 5 yards of assembly trench occupied.

8. **ALLOTMENT OF TRENCHES FOR "IN" AND "OUT" COMMUNICATION.**
See Map "D". This will entail considerable
digging and the use of the trench tramway as a
C.T. It is apparently never used as a trench
tramway and will require clearing of mud.

9. **AIDPOSTS.** No suitable dug-outs were found. 4 Aidposts will
require to be constructed, in each case near
Battalion Battle H.Q. The sites selected place
these near "OUT" C.Ts in most cases.

10. A report on necessary screening will follow, after
a further reconnaissance of the line has been made.

11. A reconnaissance with a view to selecting tracks across
country so that troops may avoid main roads will be
made later, and a report rendered.

GShoed
Brigadier General,
Commanding 168th. Infantry Brigade.

15th. March 1917.

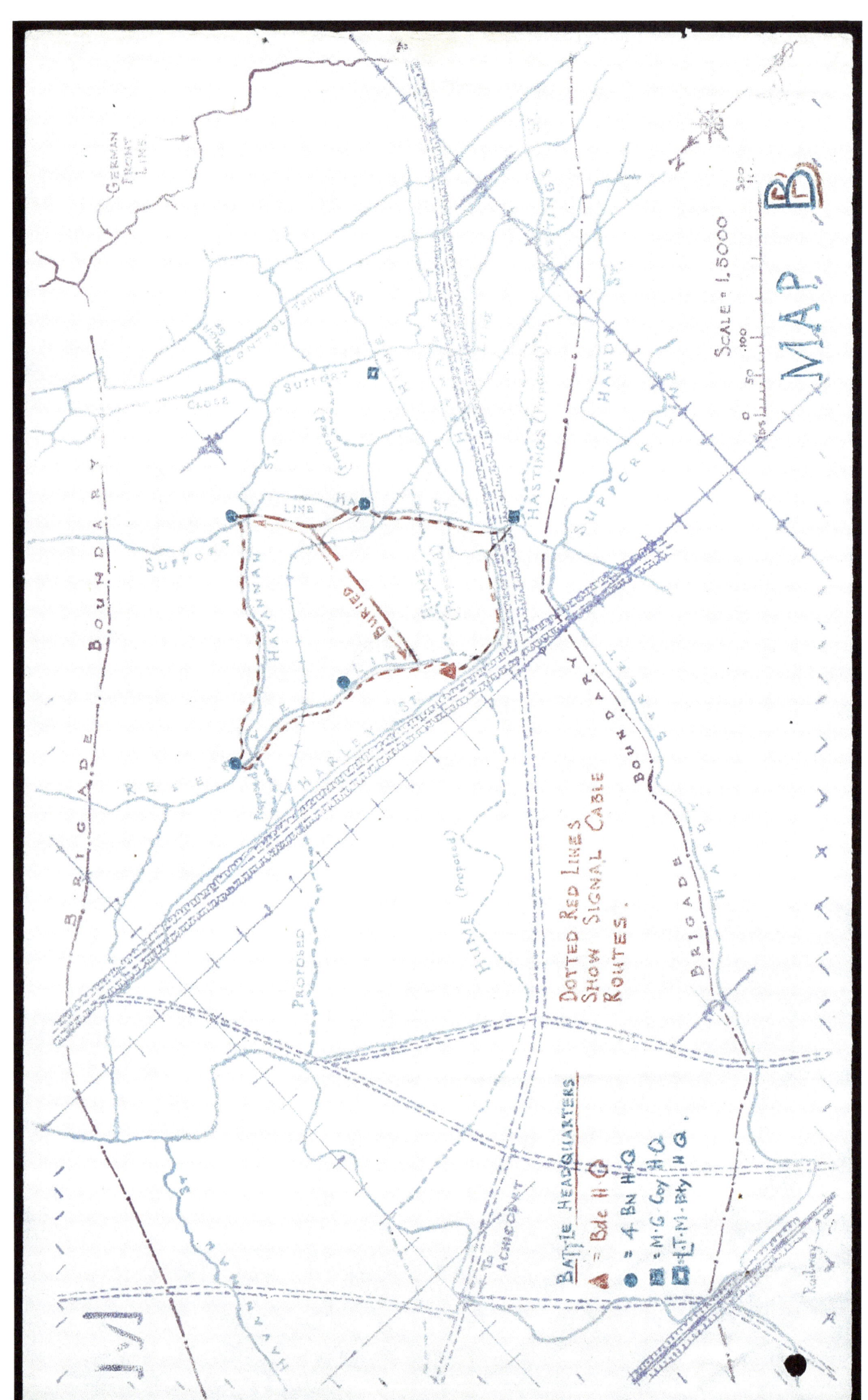

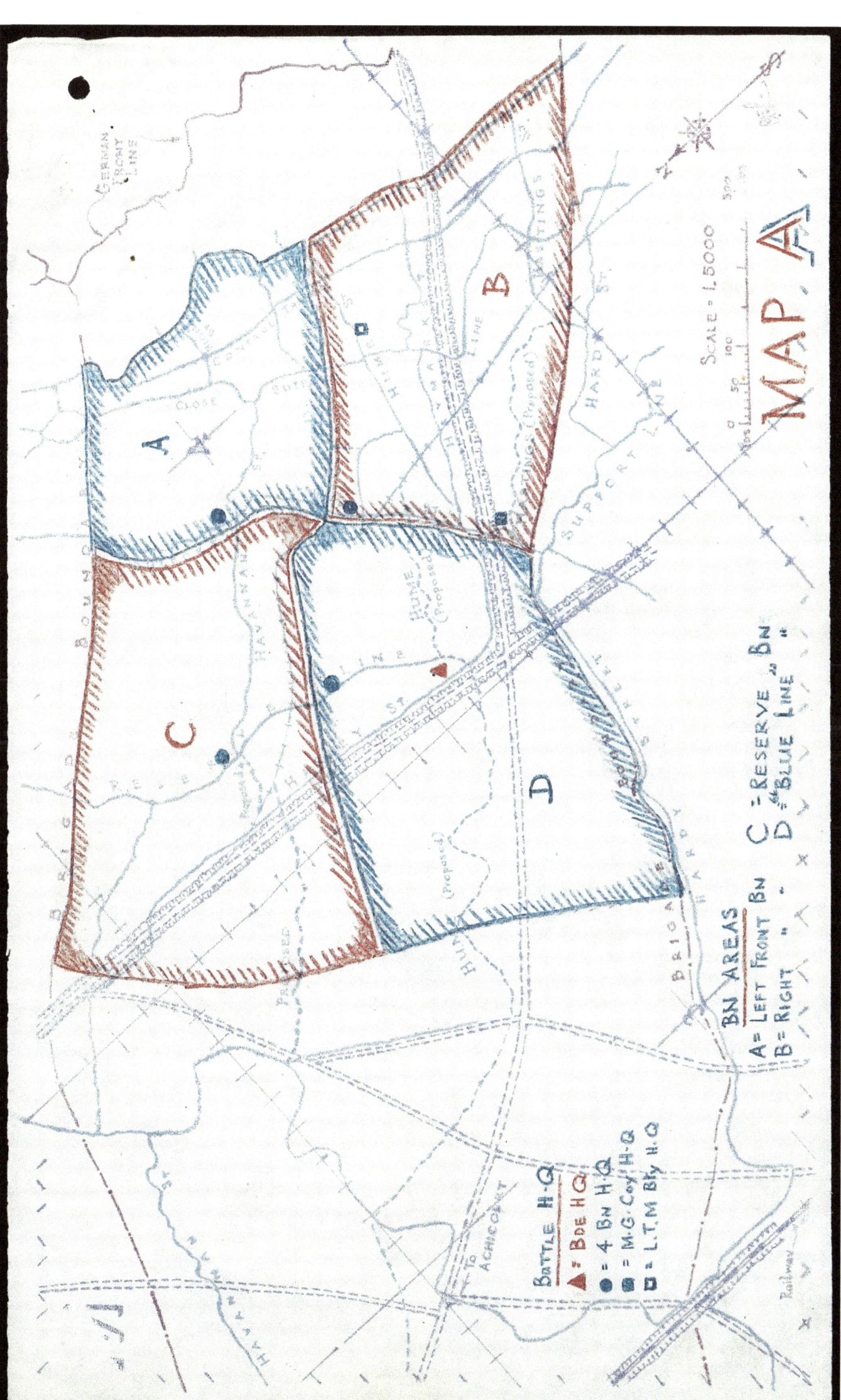

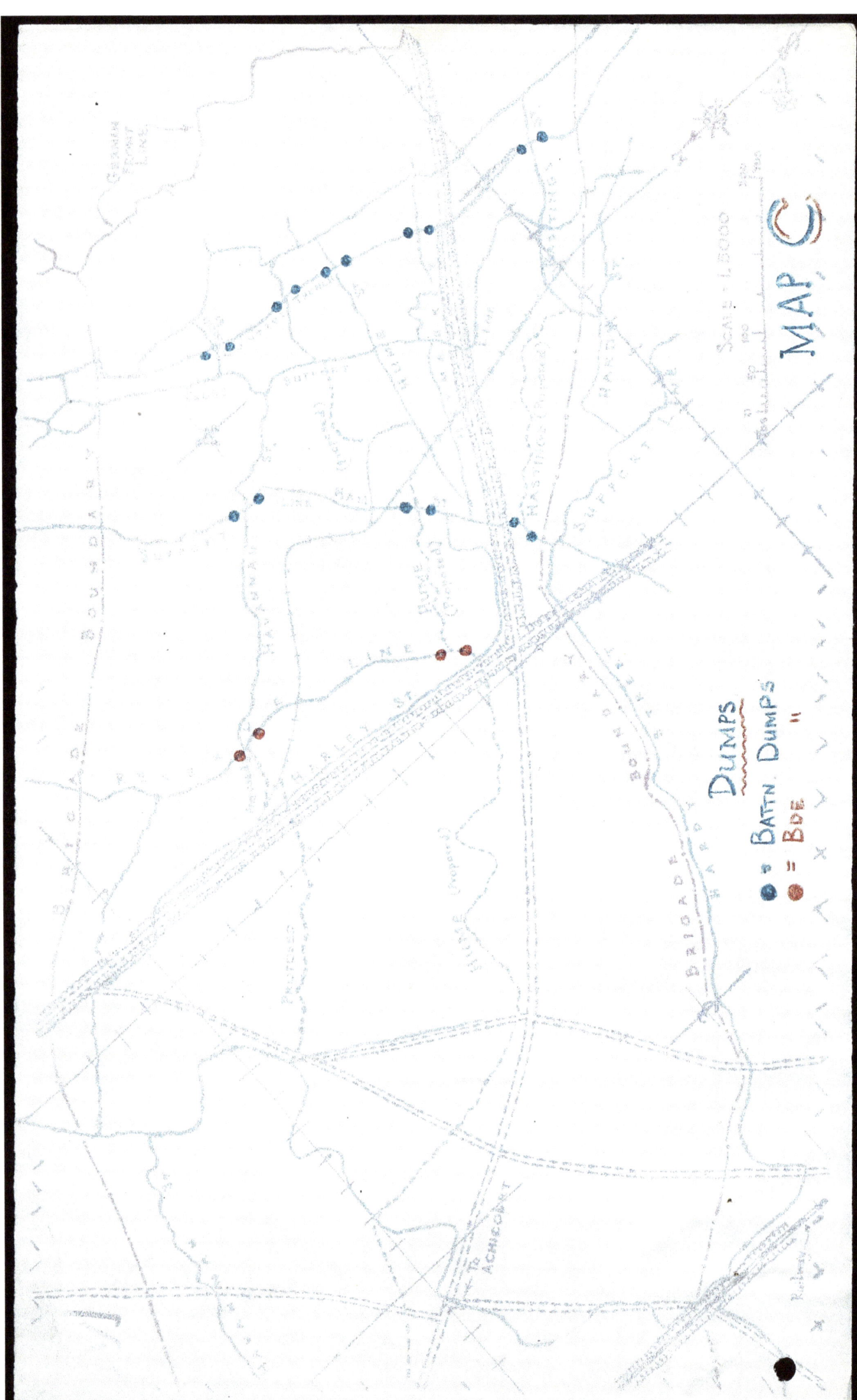

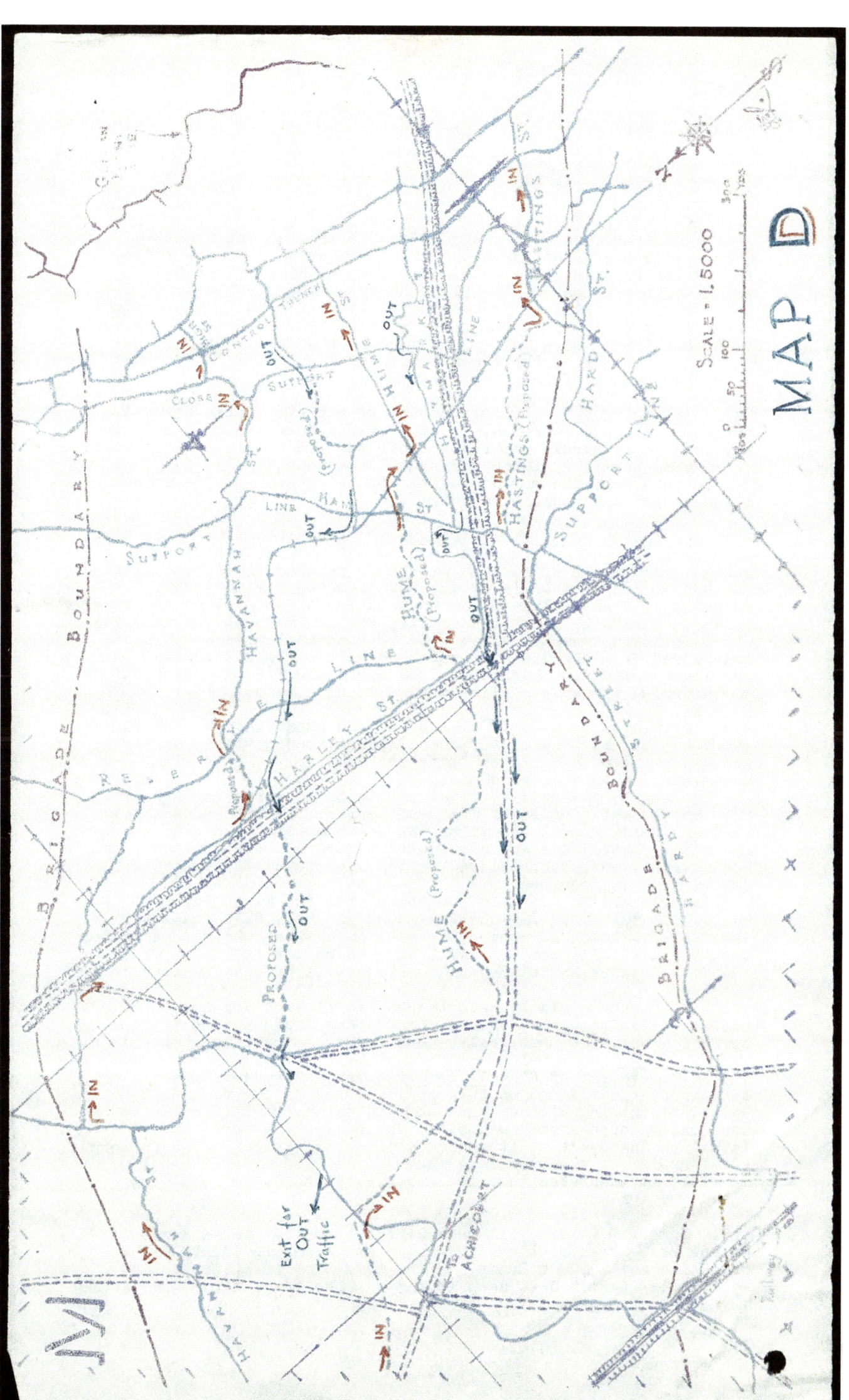

SECRET.

Headquarters.

56th. Division.

G. 589.

GA 22
16.3.17

In accordance with instructions, I carried out to-day a preliminary reconnaissance of the area allotted to the 167th. Inf. Brigade for assembly etc. previous to the contemplated offensive operations on the VIIth Corps front.

I was not able to do as much as I would have liked, owing principally to the very bad state of the trenches and also to the fact that there was a relief going on at the same time.

As a result of the reconnaissance, I was able to condense a certain amount of information.

(a). <u>Improving C.T's.</u> This cannot be satisfactorily carried out until the weather improves. At present, they are knee deep in mud ; there is hardly any revettment, and the sides have fallen in to such an extent that the berm has "disappeared".

Apart from their bad condition, the existing C.T's seem adequate for the needs of a Brigade.

(b). <u>Provision of Assembly Trenches.</u> I was not able to go into much detail, but I saw enough to be sure that, with improved weather, there are sufficient existing trenches (including disused boyaux) to form the basis of the requirements for assembly purposes. I would like C.O's to be able to reconnoitre the areas in which they will have to assemble, and to work out the details.

The main drawback appears to be that the whole area is overlooked from BEAURAINS in which there are still several prominent buildings which doubtless conceal O.P's and which should be destroyed by Heavy Artillery fire as soon as possible.

(c). <u>Provision of H.Q's.</u> These require attention generally. The dug-outs allotted as Advanced Brigade Headquarters require strutting and more earth as "bursters" on top. Otherwise, accommodation appears adequate.

Owing to the relief, I was unable to go very thoroughly into the question of Battalion Headquarters, except to ascertain that in their present condition the Headquarters allotted to assaulting Battalions are quite unsuitable. Alternative Headquarters were reconnoitred, which seem suitable, but much improvement is required.

There are no suitable "Dug-outs" for the Right Support Battalion, but a big dug-out was found in GREEN STREET about M.9.b.40.10. which is apparently very expansive, but has no timber work in it at all, and this will have to be put in hand at once. The Left Support Battalion Headquarters will have to be considerably improved.

So far as could be ascertained, sufficient dug-out accommodation <u>of sorts</u> exists for Company Headquarters in the forward areas, but practically none for the Supporting Battalions.

(d). <u>Improvement of Signal Communication.</u> Very little could be definitely ascertained on this point, owing to the fact that the Battn. Signalling Officer knew nothing of the work that has been done under Corps arrangements. The cables are buried up to Battalion Headquarters (the same as Advanced Brigade Headquarters), but I could not discover very much else.

It is suggested that the A.D.A.S. VIIth Corps should be asked for a report.

(e). <u>Dumps.</u> This will be a difficult matter to deal with unless Horse Transport can be guaranteed along the ACHICOURT - BEAURAINS and BUCQUOY Roads. The tram-line is at present a myth, being buried 3-ft deep in mud. The track along HOPE STREET is now non-existant.

(2).

(e). Cont'd.

At present, I consider the most suitable place for the Brigade Dump is just behind the point where HOPE STREET crosses the BUCQUOY Road, which at that point gives about 8-ft. of cover.

Battalion Dumps will have to be selected near Battalion Headquarters.

(f).   Bridges and Ladders.   Owing to the exposed nature of the area, it was not possible to judge how many bridges would be required, nor could any definite idea be arrived at as to the number of ladders that may be necessary.

(g).   Communication Trenches.   GREEN STREET appears to have been allotted as an "Out" trench - and HOPE STREET as an "In" trench, but this question was notv fully gone into.

(h).   Aid Posts.   This question has not yet been gone into.

(i).   Screening.   As stated previously, the whole area is under observation from BEAURAINS, but very little has been done in the way of screening.

The BUCQUOY Road might very usefully be screened throughout, but it will be a big job.

In conclusion, I consider that it is essential that opportunities should be given soon for C.O's, M.G. Company Commanders, T.M. Battery Commanders, Signalling and Intelligence Officers etc., to get up to the line and work out their requirements in detail, and it is suggested that some arrangements should be made for them to go to DAINVILLE some afternoon, remain there over night, and carry out their reconnaissances next day.

Brigadier-General,
Commanding 167th. Inf. Brigade.

15/3/17.

First Series

W 74—664 250,000 3/15 L.S. & Co.   Army Form W. 3091.

Cover for Documents.

Secret

Nature of Enclosures.

File A.2.

Offensive Operations on VII Corps front.

Correspondence with Corps.

1917 MAR

Bate 14/3/17

_____

Notes, or Letters written.

SECRET   File A2

56th Division No. G.A.41

VIIth Corps.

In continuation of my No. G.A.9 of 14th inst., I have consulted my Div. M.G.Officer, whose opinion agrees with mine, viz: That the angle of safety of M.G.Fire would not permit of these guns being able to keep to the same barrage lines as the Artillery, though there would be no objection to their bringing indirect fire on to areas or targets further removed.

I also think that there is some danger of guns working this barrage scheme being knocked out, and I would prefer to sacrifice the small additional advantage they might give to our attack in favour of keeping them in a safe position, preferably on packs and ready to be sent up rapidly in case they were needed.

Sa a. Hull

Head Qrs. 56th Divn.
18th March, 1917.

Major-General,
Commanding 56th Division.

Sir,
This has been sent.
GA 10 enclosed please?

JD
16/3

They have it
WJ

"C" Form
MESSAGES AND SIGNALS.

Army Form C. 2123.
(In books of 100.)

Prefix......... Code YER Words 21

Received From GLO By Aboy

Sent, or sent out At YER ...III.17

Office Stamp.

Charges to collect

Service Instructions GLO

Handed in at .... Office 8.15 m. Received 8.31 m.

TO 56 Bde

Sender's Number	Day of Month	In reply to Number		AAA
775	18			
How	soon	may	I	expect
plan	asked	for	in	file
A	to	9	GCR	604/136
of	13th	inst	aaa	Please
submit	in	duplicate		

G386

FROM PLACE & TIME Seventh Corps. 7.50 pm

Secret

VIIth Corps.   56th Division G.A.10.

1.   The German Line.

The German position opposite our front consists of
two systems of trenches, supported by the Villages of MERCATEL
and NEUVILLE VITASSE, which are both prepared for defence.
About 2 miles East of his second system is the Hindenburg line
which is connected to it at TELEGRAPH HILL by the COJEUL
SWITCH.   The first and second systems are heavily wired.

The first system is visible from our positions, but
there is no direct observation on the second till the first
is captured.

2.   The British Line.

Our own system of trenches consists of three lines,
firing, support and reserve lines, and varies from 400^X to
150^X from the German front line.   Our own wire is very thick
and its removal will require some thought, probably in places
it will have to be blown up.

3.   The Objects of the 56th Division are :-

(a).   To capture the German first line system between M.16.a.9.3.
and M.11.a.8.9.; this includes the village of BEAURAINS.

(b).   To capture the first line of the German second system
between M.23.a.3.4. and M.18.b.1.2., and both lines of the same
system between M.23.a.35.70 and M.17.c.95.15., i.e., the redoubt
on the MERCATEL - BEAURAINS Road.

(c).   To capture the second line of the German second system
between M.23.a.35.25. and M.18.d.3.6., also in conjunction with
the 14th Division to capture NEUVILLE VITASSE.

(d).   In conjunction with the 30th Division to capture MERCATEL,
and to push out troops on to the high ground in M.25.d. M.26.c. &
d. to link up with the 14th Division on the HENIN - WANCOURT Line.

2.

4. As regards 3 (a) & (b) I intend to attack on a front of two Brigades with the third Brigade in Divisional Reserve.

If this attack is successful I intend to use the third Brigade for objectives (c) & (d), but it must be borne in mind that this Brigade, or some of it, may have to be used in getting our first two objectives, especially if BEAURAINS and the German second system are strongly held; it must also be remembered that there is no direct observation in the second system till the first is captured, and consequently a good deal of uncut wire is certain to be met with.

5. On the capture of the German first system various strong points will be constructed, but it is not possible yet to designate these or to go into details of the attack as the front has only been taken over to-day and reconnaissances have yet to be made.

6. I attach a sketch showing my proposals for the assembly of the troops.

Head Qrs. 56th Divn.
14th March, 1917.

Major-General,
Commanding 56th Division.

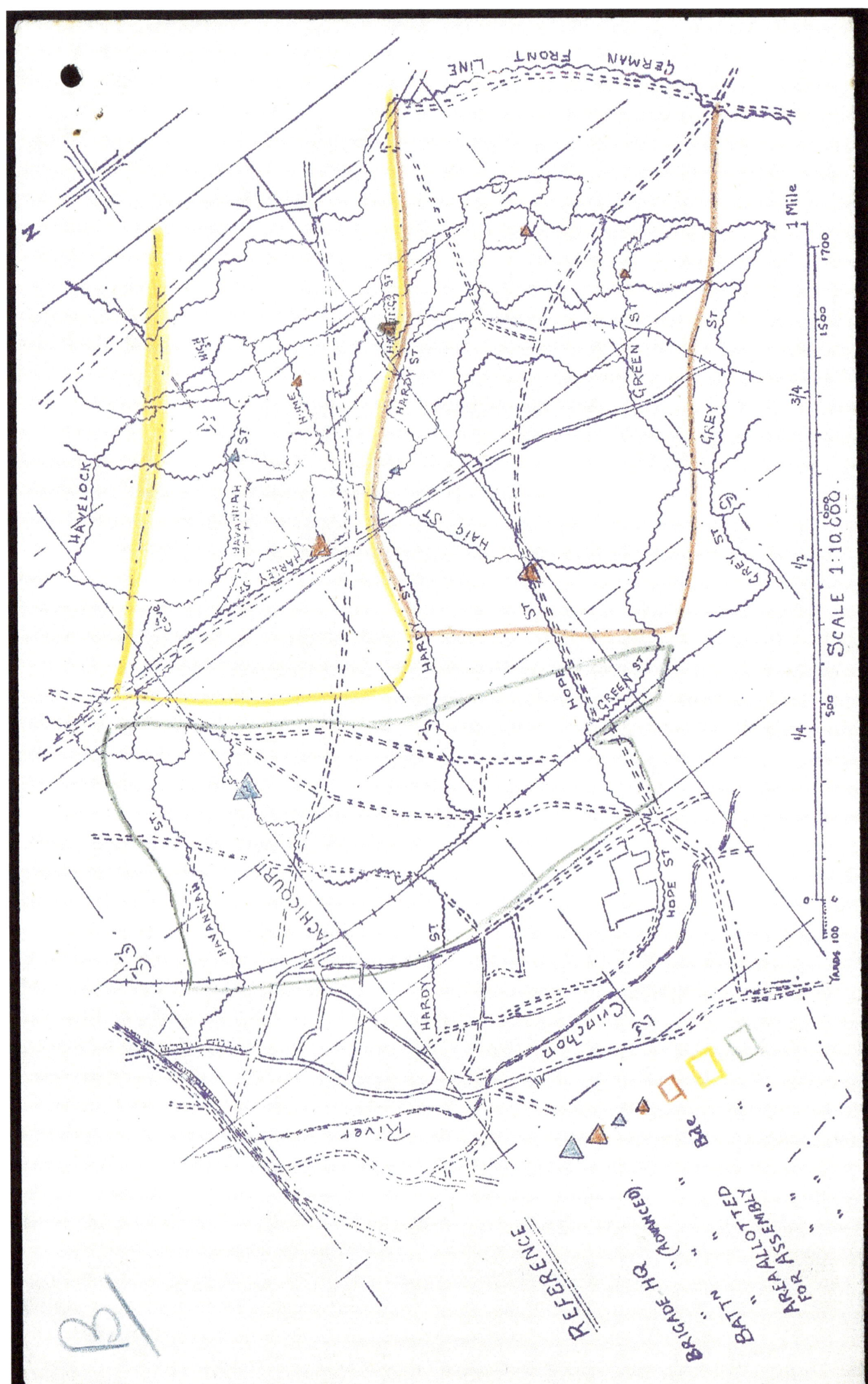

SECRET

56th Division No. 9A.11.

VII Corps.

Reference File A.

I should be glad if you would inform me of the number

of   Heavy Trench Mortars
        Medium   "   "

which will be allotted to cover the front of this Division.

Blakenham M.G.

Major-General,

Commanding 56th Division

Head Qrs. 56th Divn.
14th March, 1917.

Secret

VIIth Corps.   56th Divn. No. 9A.9.

With reference to your No. G.C.R. 604/131.

In order to save delay I am putting forward at once my own views on the scheme, but would like them to be considered as provisional until I have had the opportunity of consulting my Div. M.G.Officer after he has studied the ground.

My opinion is as follows :-

(a). There would be no objection to the barrage being placed on the German front line provided that the enemy was so "drilled" beforehand by spasmodic barrages during the 72 hours Artillery bombardment that he would not regard the first lift as an indication of impending attack.

(b). I have not yet been informed of the Artillery plan, but I presume that the guns will lift at Zero and consequently our infantry will be at that hour as close as they can get to the barrage, and will keep advancing close under it.

   I do not think that the margin of safety of machine guns will allow of their barrage invariably coinciding with that of the Artillery.

(c). I presume that the lettering on the map means that the machine gun barrage commences at A_1 and moves forward to A etc., and not that these are fixed belts of fire, as in that case the barrage would appear to be rather thin.

(d). I notice that the barrage by the Left Division crosses my front; I do not think this is sound, as I should be unable to control it.

(e). I consider that it would be better not to move any of these barrage guns forward until the capture of the second objective had been obtained. They would be furnished by my Divisional M.G.Coy. which I should prefer to keep in hand. Once the second objective had been reached, they could come into action East of BEAURAINS, but in the

/event

2.

event of failure any move before that time would probably
lead to confusion and congestion.

Head Qrs. 56th Divn.
14th March, 1917.

Sd A. Hull
Major-General,
Commanding 56th Division.

Reference proposed Scheme for an Indirect Machine M. Gun Barrage on the Corps front to assist the advance of the Infantry: and General Hull's remarks.

Confidential

1. <u>To drill the Hun into our barrage. i.e. night firing</u>

One or two carefully chosen places could never be fired at for two or three weeks before the attack, and the remainder of the back of the enemy's front line liberally sprinkled by day and night.

2 & 3. <u>Margin of Safety</u>

I do not quite understand the Scheme, but taking it that the centre division only supplies the guns for the two groups of eight in Square M3.D., I do not make the angle of safety sufficient when our troops are at A1 in red and the barrage is at A in red. This barrage is intended to creep until our troops are at B1 in blue when the barrage would be at B in blue. The angle of safety is then correct.

4. <u>Guns of the Left Division firing over our front</u>

What control has the Centre Divisional Commander over these guns? Is a time limit to be arranged?

5. I rather doubt that this elaborate scheme has been very carefully worked out. It could only be of use in the initial stages of the attack. Personally, I am all against the craze there is at present in machine gun circles to try and turn machine guns into artillery, and try to imitate a shrapnel barrage, a very risky proceeding over attacking troops. Surely the artillery can do without machine guns help in putting up barrages and sweeping reverse slopes. The machine guns would

(see over.)

then be free to perform their proper function, i.e. consolidate ground won by the infantry, using the same principle of cross fire, as was used in the Divisional machine gun defence scheme on our late front. Any guns which would not be required for the above, could be left in some safe position, preferably on packs, so that they could be brought up rapidly in case they were needed.

Guns working this barrage scheme would be liable to be knocked out, and thus could not be available for the Brigadier's and Divisional Commanders' reserve of fire power.

E.C.S. Tivers Major
D.M.G.O.

16-3-17

General Staff remarks.

1. Shell the Hun into our barrage i.e. night firing

2. What margin of safety there is.

3. Barrage appears to be rather thin, unless Creeping barrage is intended.

4. Does not care for guns of left division firing over our front.

5. Would like major-general to render an appreciation of scheme.

"C" Form (Duplicate).
MESSAGES AND SIGNALS.

Army Form C.2...
(In books of 50's in duplicate.)
No. of Message ....

| | Charges to Pay. £ s. d. | Office Stamp. |

Service Instructions.

Handed in at .... Office .... m. Received .... m.

TO

Sender's Number	Day of Month	In reply to Number	AAA
9710			

Ref GOR 604/131 aaa For left
group on PARA 3 read
Right group

(301)

FROM
PLACE & TIME: 7 Corps

14th Division.
~~30th Division.~~
56th Division.
M.G.O. VII Corps.

Reference File A.

1. To assist the advance of the Infantry, a proposal has been put forward for an indirect Machine Gun Barrage on the Corps front.

   Attached Map shows the proposed scheme.

2. The number of guns necessary would be 80.

3. The ~~left~~ *right* group of 16 guns could possibly be taken on by one of the Machine Gun Companies of the XVIIIth Corps, this would free the guns of the Right Brigade of the 30th Division for forward movement.

4. This barrage could be used before and during the advance from the assembly positions to the second objective.

5. The objects of the barrage will be as follows :-

   (a) To keep under fire trenches, wire, etc. destroyed during the preliminary bombardment which cannot be engaged by direct machine gun fire.

   (b) To increase the effect of the shrapnel barrage.

   (c) To keep down hostile machine gun and rifle fire in the trenches.

   (d) To assist in repelling any counter attack.

6. To ensure the maximum effect with the fewest number of guns Divisions would have to detail an experienced Machine Gun Officer to work out all details for his Divisional front in conjunction with the Corps Machine Gun Officer.

   The attached Map shows in Red Marked 'A' the position of the barrage at Zero, and in Green marked 'B' the position

/ when

2.-

when the Infantry have gained the first objective.

Several guns will be able to continue the barrage for a short time during the advance of the Infantry to the second objective, other positions will have to be cut out and new ones substituted in the first objective from which direct fire can be obtained.

7. Since the control of the barrage on each Divisional front is entirely in the hands of the Divisional Commander, the lifts on each Divisional Front must be worked out to synchronize with the movement of the Artillery barrage, subject to the safety limits necessary/for this form of machine gun fire.

Divisional Commanders will please give the proposal their consideration and forward their views at as early a date as possible.

~~A case return attached here.~~

Ack'd

13th March 1917.

Brigadier-General,
General Staff, VIIth Corps.

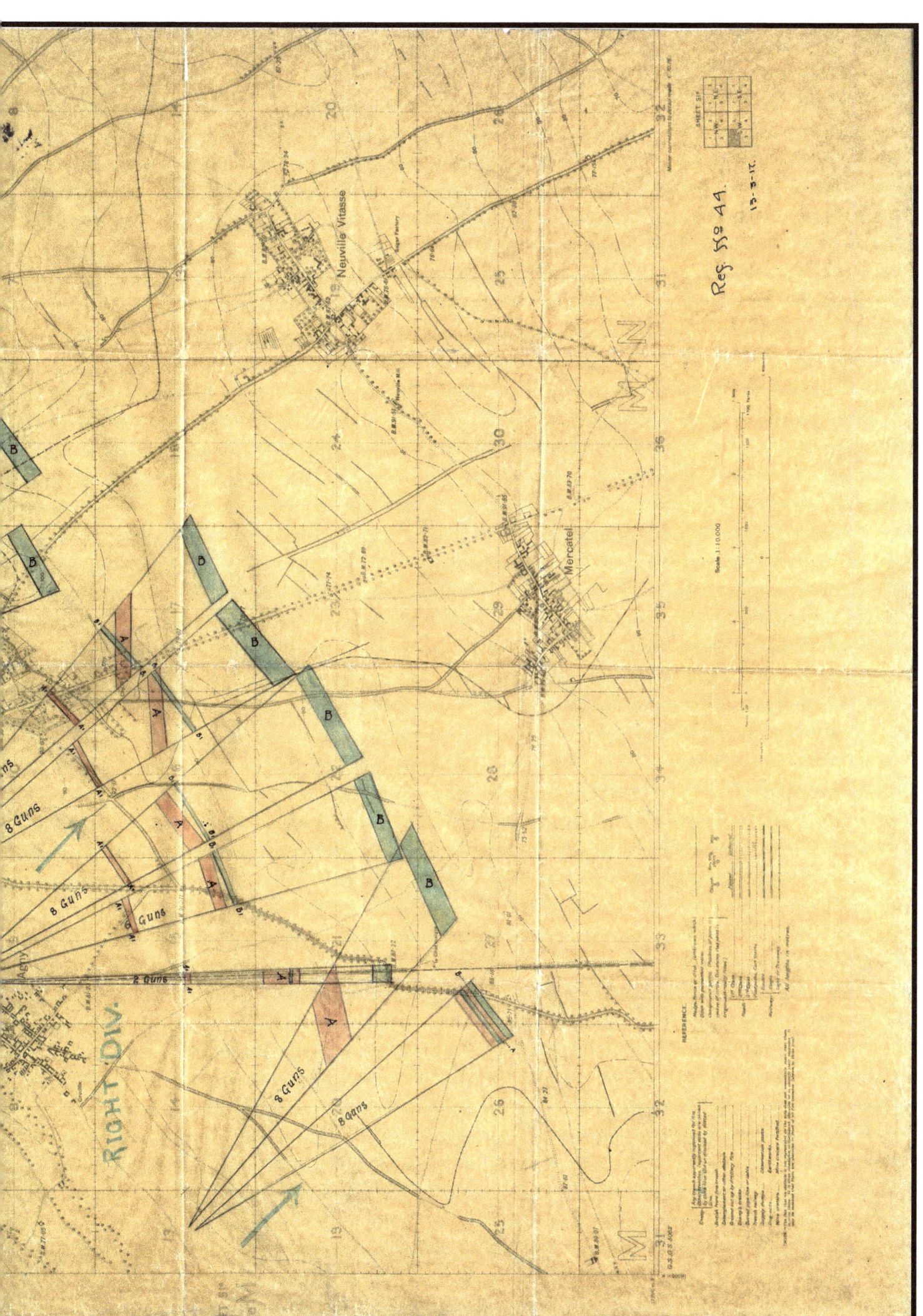

www.ingramcontent.com/pod-product-compliance
Lightning Source LLC
Chambersburg PA
CBHW081424160426
43193CB00013B/2184